Satisfy Their Unmet Need

STUN!
Selling

by Paul Russell

STUNselling.com

ISBN-13: 978-0-9967881-0-6 (ej4, LLC)

Edited by Alana Muller.
Cover and graphic design by Pete Nelson.
Layout and text design by Joann Bittel.
Cover photography by Thorsten Fraley.

Dedication

This book is dedicated to the thousands of managers and sales people at Pepsi-Cola Bottlers, Anheuser-Busch Wholesalers and Dr Pepper Snapple who, since 1985, both learned from and taught me about their businesses, their customers, the objections they had to overcome and the obstacles they faced.

Acknowledgments

First to Ryan Eudy, CEO and now part owner of my company, ej4. Among all that Ryan has given me are two invaluable things. First, he has provided me peace of mind that my company no longer requires me; he has it under control. Second, because of the first, he has given me the invaluable gift of time. Time to write, time to think, time to experiment.

Beryl Raff, CEO of Helzberg Diamonds, is next. Smarter and more accomplished than I, Beryl has given me insights that I never could have otherwise imagined. She works for Warren Buffett who hired her after a half-day interview. If you want to know about the amazing Ms. Raff, Google her. Hers is a remarkable story.

Next, oddly, is my former business partner, Dr. Kenneth Carleton Cooper, PhD. He gave me the courage to borrow more money than I ever thought I could, should or would put at risk to buy his shares of ej4 to become sole owner. I grew immeasurably from the opportunity he gave me. Thanks, Dr. Ken.

And thanks also to my ex-wife, Debi Russell, for many things like doing the primary raising of our two great kids, Cianán and Megan, while I traveled the country and the world earning money and building our foundation for the future. But, strangely enough, the greatest thanks is for one amazing gesture she made after we divorced: Loaning me the money from our property settlement to finance the debt to buy the other half of the company from Dr. Cooper. She didn't have to do that and I know her advisor said not to. She did it anyway. Bravo. Oh, and that also made it possible for me to later fund college expenses for our two beautiful grandsons; an unexpected dividend from her gesture.

Next to the founders of Padgett-Thompson Seminars, Dr. Harold Finch and George Robertson (the name of the company came from the maiden names of their wives so that seminar attendees would never be disappointed that the company namesakes didn't show up to present the seminars because they didn't exist — did you follow that?). I presented over 800 seminars for these two and learned an amazing amount from having done so. But, surprisingly, the greatest benefit I got from them was learning how to set goals for myself. The fact that I could never hope to achieve those goals as long as I remained affiliated with them gave me the courage to leave and start the Russell Training Group, Inc. Who knows where I would be today had I not taken that leap?

To Kevin Silva, then the Executive Director of the Pepsi-Cola Management Institute, I owe great thanks because it was Kevin who gave me the business foundation for RTG, Inc., to pay the bills. When he moved to MasterCard International, he brought me along. Later, Anita Marx, then the Executive Director of Anheuser-Busch's Beer Marketing Management Development, showed a faith in me that strengthened both RTG, Inc. and me immensely. Others at A-B include Mike Brooks, Jim Hunter and Mark Danner. At Pepsi-Cola General Bottlers, it was Bob Cushing, Brud LeTourneau and many others. At Buffalo Rock Corporation, it was Jimbo Lee and Jim Reddinger. At Pepsi, Barbara Burek. Thanks

ACKNOWLEDGMENTS

to Dr Pepper Snapple Group CEO, Larry Young, who recommended me to EVPHR, Larry Solomon, who hired us to set up DPS Campus and innovate with their coaches. To the many people at MasterCard including Laura Keenan and Mike Calamari and former CEO Pete Hart who was an inspiration. Also to Cheryl Roberts, Managing Director and Global Head of HR for UBS and Steven Baird who, at UBS, wrote me a note I'll never forget saying, "You are a legend around here," and got me the most amazing consulting assignment that I ever had with a wayward executive that I cannot name here. More thanks to Ace Hardware, Ralph D'Onofrio and Fredricka Brecht at Pennzoil, Sherrill Crivellone at Citadel, Amaranth, Dolly Madison and many others, thanks for believing in me to deliver on my promises when dealing with your teams. Mike Jerrick gave me confidence when we both worked at KMBC-TV Channel 9 in Kansas City where I was groomed to follow him (even though I didn't) before he got his dream job in New York City. At Josten's, thanks to Larry Pirnie, Paul Erickson, Rex Howard, Charlie Herrmann, Dave Ramberg, Fred Bjork, and Wendell "The Silver Fox" Dayton. At Vance Publishing, Jim Staudt and Jan Kessinger. Thanks, finally, to Paul Wineman who selflessly taught me how to negotiate for win/win outcomes.

Thanks to ej4's Pete Nelson for illustrating my words and thoughts and to Thorsten Fraley for shooting and editing my words and Pete's graphics and improving with every new video. Also at ej4, thanks to Kathy Irish, Tom Lynch and Mandy Owen and all the rest. You and others made the company great and continue to do so.

Last, to Alana Muller of Coffee Lunch Coffee, *coffeelunchcoffee.com*. On this book, I had more false starts than you can imagine. I could not lock down the process to get it written. Alana helped me find my way. She kept me on track. She held me accountable. She got me to agree to deadlines (and a goal without a deadline is just a dream). She edited, suggested, critiqued, praised and smiled throughout. She STUNned me before she knew what STUN was. Thanks, Alana.

Table of Contents

You can
STUN!

My name is completely irrelevant. My story, however, is relevant to you and can be of great value if you want to become a better and more successful salesperson. Regardless of whether you sell products or services, regardless of whether you have the lowest price, regardless of your current market share—regardless of all these things and more, you can become more successful if you will STUN your prospects. That is: Satisfy Their Unmet Needs.

Upon graduation from Kansas City, Missouri's Ruskin High School in 1966, I was hired by Commerce Bank of Kansas City to come spend two weeks selling checking account services to my classmates. I had been the student body president and the bank must have figured that I would be a natural. I wasn't. I was not comfortable cold calling people. I could not close. I was afraid to ask for the order. The idea of hearing "No" kept me from asking; I feared—as many do—rejection. I didn't know how to open a sales presentation... to set the hook. I didn't understand objections or know how to overcome them. I thought all selling was pushy and, somehow, "sleazy."

I didn't get into the colleges I wanted: Harvard, Yale and Princeton. Coming from a broken home and growing up with a family who were not my legal guardians, I found I could not qualify for in-state tuition to a Missouri state institution because my legal guardian lived in a different state. Through the good graces of my brother's wife, I got a late admission into a small school in Kansas: Kansas State College of Pittsburg (since renamed Pittsburg State University).

While there, I worked 45 hours per week at KOAM-TV and worked my way up to the post of managing editor of the student newspaper, *The Collegio*, but I often skipped class. I got fired from KOAM (a long story) and spent time being unemployed having low confidence in myself and unable to sell my skills to a prospective employer. An interesting side note is this: The person hired to replace me was also fired and the person hired to replace him was none other than Brian Williams of NBC News fame.

Later, I was hired as the yearbook sales representative for the Josten's/American Yearbook Company, first in Denver and later in Milwaukee. Me? A salesperson? I was only OK at that job. When it came to service after the sale I was great. However, the actual selling process was a struggle for me. I was still afraid to risk hearing that "No" from a prospect, so I would keep on selling and selling without closing. I guess I somehow assumed that my prospects would become so convinced of the wisdom of working with me that at some point in my elongated presentation they would hold up a hand to stop me and say, "Paul, say no more. This sounds great. Where do I sign?"

That never happened. Not once.

Over time, however, I got better. At Josten's, I learned a lot from a trainer named Dave Ramberg and my sales manager, Tom Jenz. Later, I changed careers and entered the training field with a seminar company called Padgett Thompson. While the owners there, Harold Finch and George Robertson, taught me everything I needed to know about how to set goals for myself, they put me in an environment where I could never hope to achieve any of them. Soon thereafter, I received an offer from Kevin Silva at the Pepsi-Cola Management Institute to become a contract faculty member teaching selling skills to Pepsi-Cola Bottler reps across the United States and beyond. I kept learning.

Later, Anheuser-Busch offered me a contract consulting position and training opportunity at their Beer Marketing Management Department. I learned even more from Anita Marx, Mike Brooks, Jim Hunter and many others. Opportunities arose at MasterCard International, UBS, Ace Hardware, Dolly Madison Bakeries, Sara Lee Bakeries, Guys Foods, Eagle Claw Fishing Tackle, Pennzoil, Vance Publishing Corporation and quite a few others and I learned more at every step.

I became a very good seller. I once closed a $1.5 million deal with a direct close made to a committee. My associates who sat on my left and right were petrified, but I was cool and confident. Turns out, after having been born with absolutely no selling skills whatsoever, I have learned a thing or two about how to sell. Selling is a process and, once learned and mastered, it is a life skill of the most rewarding kind I know.

But, around the turn of the century, it occurred to me that my business model was going to become very similar to Kodak's. If I kept hanging onto my old way of doing things — even though I was by all measures quite successful — I was going to fail. So, I partnered up with

Dr. Ken Cooper and we proceeded to reinvent the training business for entities such as Pepsi, Anheuser-Busch, Dr Pepper and others. We started the company ej4.

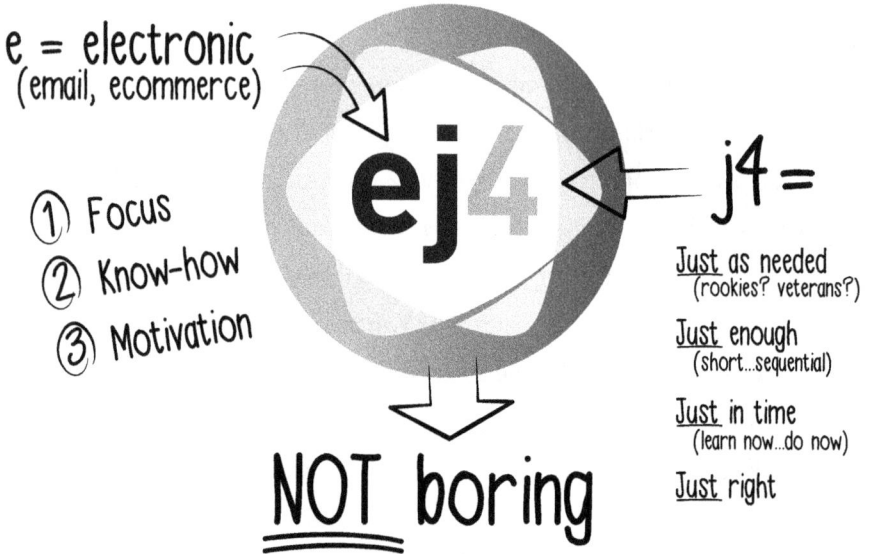

e = electronic
(email, ecommerce)

① Focus
② Know-how
③ Motivation

ej4

j4 =

<u>Just</u> as needed
(rookies? veterans?)

<u>Just</u> enough
(short...sequential)

<u>Just</u> in time
(learn now...do now)

<u>Just</u> right

<u>NOT</u> boring

I am often asked about how we named ej4. The e stands for "electronic" much as it does the terms "email" or "ecommerce." As we tried to figure out how to STUN our customers, we first admitted that they needed faster response times with training initiatives; with that, I remember writing "Just in Time" on a flip chart. Additionally, we knew they needed more advanced training for their veterans and more basic training for their rookies so I wrote "Just as Needed" on the chart. Next, we agreed that their employees had very short attention spans so I wrote "Just Enough" on the chart. My memory is vivid about this next point: We agreed that training couldn't be boring. So, finally, seeing the progress of "Justs" on the chart, I wrote "Just Right."

From somewhere, Einstein's "e=mc2" entered my head and, mimicking that, I wrote ej4 on the chart. A quick Google search revealed that the web address ej4.com was available and the entity had a name.

The name was based upon the unmet needs of our customers. Even though I had yet to create the acronym STUN, that was what our business name was all about: Satisfy Their Unmet Needs. It was to become the foundation for our success.

I learned a lot from Dr. Cooper; we parted company when I bought him out. The entire ej4 team seemed quite pleased having a single owner rather than two and they all stayed aboard.

We built a thriving business at ej4. Ryan Eudy became the CEO, Tom Lynch deftly handled technology, Kathy Irish ran this and that with her remarkable attitude and others like Pete Nelson chipped in with innovative creativity to make us a leader in our field.

At ej4, we are a leading producer of short business training video segments, sequentially arranged into a curriculum format. For Dr Pepper Snapple, as an example, we helped to create a state of the art coaching system under the guidance of their Executive Vice President of Human Resources, Larry Solomon. Now retired and consulting for other firms while writing a new book, Solomon saw what could be accomplished by turning his supervisors into coaches. This was a theme that DPS Chairman and CEO Larry Young believed in and preached for a very long time. I know because I worked with Young decades earlier when he was an executive at Pepsi-Cola General Bottlers where I worked as a consultant and sales trainer.

Solomon's segments were delivered at very low cost to every manager in the DPS system and they helped turn that group into true coaches who, in turn, increased revenue and decreased expenses with a renewed efficiency. As supervisors they were good, but as coaches they were great. Dr Pepper Snapple paid us to do this work and it delivered to them a solid ROI—Return on Investment.

At ej4, we built on Solomon's efforts and created a generic version of the same role-changing skills for delivery to some of our other clients. The goal was to make their organizations more profitable (or, in the case of not-for-profit enterprises, more successful) by following up on our unshakable belief that training should teach learners how to effectively increase revenue or reduce expenses, or both.

6]

Recently, as a result of having our low-cost training platform, I had what I thought was a fabulous idea. It turned out to be not such a fabulous idea because we couldn't get it closed. There are several reasons why we couldn't get it closed. I was seduced by how much revenue we had in our pipeline, but ultimately disappointed by how little of that money made it to our bottom line. We just couldn't get the deals closed. Pipeline money is worth nothing; bottom line money is worth everything. Here's the scenario:

Years ago, when we were headquartered in another town, I was approached by the local Chamber of Commerce about joining their organization. Partially because I wanted to know "what's in it for me?"

if we joined and partially because I wanted to see how good a salesperson their representative was, I asked the simple question, "Why should we join?"

The answer I received from the young man who called upon us was that we would be helping to make our city a better place to operate a business. I pressed him, "Yes, but what's in it for us? What benefits do we receive for giving you our money — other than helping to make this suburb a better place to do business?"

"You get to network with other businesses and make contacts that way," he said. He didn't really have any more of an answer for me. The conversation continued...

> Paul: *"Will we, for example, gain access to a group of employers who have banded together to gain lower cost health insurance like the big employers get?"*
>
> Chamber Rep: *"No."*

I was revealing to him an unmet need but it went over his head.

> Paul: *"Will we, for example, gain access to a group of employers who have banded together to gain discounts on fleet insurance or office supplies?"*
>
> Chamber Rep: *"No."*

I was revealing another unmet need. He didn't hear or understand it.

> Paul: *"Well, what do we get?"*
>
> Chamber Rep: *"You would be helping to make our city a better place for your business to operate,"* he reiterated. *"And, don't forget the networking opportunities."*

He assumed that his unmet need — to make our city a better place to do business and to network with others — was my unmet need, too. It wasn't. So I pressed him.

> Paul: *"Yes, but how exactly do we benefit from that?"*

He didn't have an answer. We didn't join. That saved me $486.45.

For other reasons having nothing to do with the Chamber of Commerce, I decided to relocate ej4 from that suburb to a newly revitalized area of neighboring Kansas City, Missouri, a fifteen minute drive from our old location. The Crossroads district of Kansas City is home to creative enterprises run by entrepreneurs like us and I believed we would gain from the "vibe" one felt when in that part of the City.

Not long after we moved, we were approached by a representative of that city's local Chamber of Commerce asking if we would like to become members. Deja vu. My new local Chamber had a couple of new answers to the "What's In It For Me?" question. There was a discount on office supplies through Staples. There was a fleet discount on vehicles if bought through a nearby Chevrolet dealer. Aflac and CBiz offered discounted services as well. This, along with networking opportunities was available to me for a cost of $550.00 annually.

However, a frustrating conversation ensued remarkably similar to my earlier experience. Then, I got an idea.

8]

"Since you have nothing specific to offer prospective members such as myself, let me suggest something. At ej4, we provide business skills training. How about buying that training from me at a deep discount and then either re-selling it or providing it free to your members? They get a tangible benefit for their membership dollars that way." I thought I had discovered an unmet need of theirs — to provide some tangible low-cost benefit of membership — that matched up with an unmet need of mine — to sell more on-line training. For the Chamber, they would be STUNned by signing more new members, increasing their membership retention rate and gaining non-dues revenue.

My thought was that providing high-value, low-cost training services to small business members of a Chamber of Commerce was a no-brainer. Everyone needs sales people who can sell more at a higher margin, supervisors who could coach teams for higher productivity, project managers who could deliver results within deadlines, interviewers who could make better hires while avoiding employment law violations, OSHA compliance training and much more. To me, this would be a great benefit that Chambers could use to grow their "business."

The person from the Chamber was enthusiastic but, as the idea when up the ladder, it died.

I decided the idea was a good one so I hired a national Chamber expert to work as a contractor to help me introduce ej4 to the Chamber world. His name is Michael Brazier and he knows Chambers of Commerce as well as anyone I ever met. He thought it was a great idea and I *knew* it was a great idea. This was one of those win/win opportunities that come along every once in a while that just make sense.

It failed. It failed miserably. And it wasn't because of Mike. We —I include myself here —couldn't make it work.

Why? We couldn't close. We had great initial interest and enthusiasm for what we were trying to do from Chamber executives across the country but we couldn't close.

The Chambers I came into contact with don't function like businesses. They're more like governments. Most of them have no strong visionary leader who decides to try something; they have committees who vacillate and ultimately —and slowly —decide to do nothing.

Our pipeline was full of Chambers that loved the idea, but we only closed two and that was not enough to sustain the expense of my consultant and my internal overhead. My management team recommended that we abandon the idea and I had to agree. My idea didn't work.

It was a good idea and still is. The problem was "Closing the Sale." As you read this book and, if you avail yourself of the opportunity to watch the companion videos, I will outline STUN, the process that I steadfastly maintain is the key to success in all ethical sales.

If you embrace STUN, you're halfway home. To get the rest of the way, you need to make effective use of many sales sub-processes or, as I refer to them in this book collectively, the STUN Toolkit. Among them is setting up closes and then closing in the right way. In addition, you need to learn the processes for handling the four unique types of objections all sellers hear. You need to determine the personality type of your prospect and adjust your sales personality to complement their buying personality. You'll learn about how to create "nod momentum." You'll learn about the staircase method of turning features into benefits. You'll learn about things I call "The Circle" and "The QuickSell" and more.

This book is part sales instruction manual, part memoir. You will notice with each STUN Tool, I provide you with a quick overview of what you'll learn, tell you The Point of each Tool, share details along with a few stories, tell you What I Would Have Done Differently had I had the Tool at my disposal earlier in my career and give you some tips for What You Should Do Right Now to gain a working command of the Tool. Each individual Tool and its accompanying process is remarkably simple and, if I explain each one correctly, you'll probably think, "Well, that's logical and it sounds like it would work," and you might even ask yourself why you didn't already think of it. The trick is to recognize the situation you are in—moment to moment to moment—in the overall sales process and know instinctively when to make use of each sub-process. That will take time and practice. Putting it all together is the most difficult part of STUN. But, one thing I know. You can do it. I know you can learn it all and, through practice, become proficient because that is what I did. I am far from being a "born seller." I learned how to sell.

What **STUN**™ Really Is

Here's What You're Going to Learn

STUN your customers. That is, Satisfy Their Unmet Needs.

When you adopt this as your sales process, you'll learn how to turn tough customers into easier customers, how to close faster, how to stop customer nibbling, how to overcome the price objection and much more. You'll be STUNned.

THE POINT

People are motivated by things that satisfy their unmet needs. Therefore, it stands to reason, they will be motivated to buy when you STUN them.

Early in my career, I had the exciting opportunity to ride along with a vast array of company reps as they made sales calls. In the car or truck, on the way to the customer's location, we'd chit chat, make a little small talk and I'd always ask the question, "What need are we selling to today?" Every time I asked the question, I got the wrong answer.

The beer guys said, "We are selling the need for an end cap display of beer in the grocery store we are about to visit." From the soft drink folks, I heard, "We are selling the need for extra facings of our new product in the cold vault of the convenience store." The bakery team told me, "We are selling the need to get our offerings in first position on the shelf." No surprise, the motor oil guys said the same thing the beer guys said. The advertising people said, "a contract." The insurance folks said, "a policy."

By the time I had heard the same general response several hundred times, I knew what the answer was going to be so I was always ready with my counter-response and next question.

"That's the need we're selling *from*," I would say. "That's *your* need. I know what you need because I know your boss and your company and your products and I know that they told you to go out and sell the display or new SKU (stock keeping unit — the new item) or whatever. What I want to know from you is not what you need but what they need." The point here is that buyers don't care what sellers need. Buyers are a very self-centered bunch — as well they should be.

Virtually every time I rejected the rep's answer to my first question, silence would fill the car. My host would adopt a stiff posture and a perplexed facial expression. These sellers, whether rookies or veterans, always looked at the prospective sale from their perspective alone. Perhaps that is why most of them disliked their customers as much as they did. They didn't think as their customers did. So when, after proposing what they had in mind from the seller's perspective, they were greeted with objection after objection. Worse, they were greeted with disinterest or, worse still, hostility. These sellers felt as if they were in a combat situation. Nobody wants to be constantly under fire.

But then, no buyer wants to be pestered by sellers who have no understanding of what their business needs to survive or thrive. No buyer wants to be sold to when the key to the sale remains unaddressed — their need for the product or the service being offered.

[13

And Then There Was Walmart... and Other Excuses to Not Buy

As a side note, during those ride alongs, I discovered the sales calls made to Walmart store managers were particularly unpopular. Nothing worked with them. In defense of Walmart managers, in their heyday, they didn't need much. Store traffic was robust and shopping carts were full.

"I need a better price," they said. "Give me a discount or get out. I don't need it. I don't want it. I don't have room for it."

You couldn't take them to lunch because it was against corporate policy. You dared not ask about their kids or their hobbies because they had been trained that such questions were manipulative ploys on

the part of evil sellers to gain an emotional edge. No matter what you asked of them, they asked even more of you to the point of making outrageous demands. The piranha had nothing on the Walmart manager when it came to nibbling. And, they would constantly threaten to throw you out of their store if you failed to meet their outsized expectations. When they threatened to give to your competition the business and space they originally offered to you, you knew they meant it. "Walmart doesn't need you," they said; "You need Walmart." Only a fool would call their bluff because to lose Walmart meant tremendous loss of volume, if not profit. Losing Walmart meant losing your job.

Store managers for other retail chains were not originally so adversarial. Those buyers hated or feared Walmart as a competitor and so you as a seller shared that feeling of disdain and fear as a point of commonality and, even if unspoken, a sense of camaraderie. Some were rude and arrogant, to be sure, but most could not match Walmart personnel for anti-social and even rude behavior. But, still, these others said, "I don't have any space," or, "I've already got one of those from your competition so I don't see why I need another one from you," or, worst of all, a flat "No."

Just "No" with no reason why or why not is the most difficult objection of all. When there is nothing to tackle, you can only flounder and floundering seldom leads to success. A real objection is so much more welcome. "I need more service," or "I need tickets to the game," or "I need a neon beer sign" (which we knew would more likely go in their home recreation room than in their store) or any of a thousand different responses all said the same thing: "No." These requests for tickets or other "goodies" are typically banned by larger corporations' policies and are usually tightly enforced. The same requests from smaller companies and especially from sole proprietors or some consumers are so common as to be pervasive. My favorite way to deal with this situation was to simply say, "I don't have tickets, but you can get them from my competition. What I do have is a traffic generating (or transaction or some other value producing) idea which they don't have. Get the tickets from them and the traffic generation opportunities (or other benefit) from me."

You can always give them more service or try for a pair of tickets or scrounge up a neon sign, but even as you provided those "perks," you knew your competitor could also say, "me too," giving you a very short-lived advantage.

But, when they want nothing, nothing helps.

WIIFM... and the Buyer?

Having been in these sellers' shoes myself, I have felt the same feelings, dealt with the same challenges, suffered the same disappointments. It always seemed to me that when buyers didn't buy they weren't doing their jobs. But, unlike many other sellers, I spent hours listening to what I heard and analyzing <u>why</u> my customers were saying these things and agonized about why these buyers behaved the way they did. Early on, I thought it was me. I wasn't as good a seller as I needed to be, I supposed. But when I compared notes with others who dealt with these same buyers, I came to the realization that what was happening to me was also happening to others. It wasn't me; it was not these other sellers. I decided it was the buyers.

They all had, I finally figured out, invisibly tattooed on their foreheads, in the largest typeface that would fit, the words, "So What?" Walmart foreheads read, "SO WHAT?!!" These buyers were, in a fashion, known to be virtually

[15

universal among us humans, asking, "What's In It For Me?" the phrase often shortened to the acronym "WIIFM?" pronounced by those who nodded knowingly as "wiff-um." We are selfish beings, we humans. We do things to cause good things to happen to us. Some of us care about the other guy, but most buyers are not coming to work each day looking for win/win outcomes. They want to — they demand to — win while caring little or nothing about what happens to everyone else.

Customer Profitability Model

That tattooed forehead vision prompted me (working with valuable input from countless others) to create what I call the CPM, or the "Customer Profitability Model." CPM is a complicated concept, but what it comes down to is one true fact: The only thing customers care about is how much profit they make — not just from one product (the one you or I are selling), but from their entire enterprise. And, like most businesses, they want to make more this year than they did last year and they'll want to make more next year than they did this year.

Realizing profitability is the buyer's goal, an insightful seller must figure out how to help their buyer achieve that profit. The answer is, vastly oversimplified (but good enough for now), they must have more revenue than they have expenses.

$$Profitability = Revenue - Expenses$$

That realization leads the thoughtful seller performing a "root cause" analysis to ask: "From where does the revenue come?" Again, oversimplified, it comes from two sources, traffic and average transaction size in dollars. It's pretty simple: Ten people spending $10 each means a revenue total of $100. In some business situations — the grocery channel comes to mind — the traffic count assumes that everyone buys something.

16]

If you go into a grocery store, virtually every time, you make a purchase. This is not true in the jewelry business. Customers go in and browse but may not actually spend any money on their first trip. When thinking about traffic, it is important to think about it the way your customer thinks about it. Good to know.

$$\text{Revenue} = \text{Traffic (\#)} \times \text{Average Transaction Size (\$)}$$

But, digging deeper, anyone analyzing this CPM must ask themselves, "From where does the traffic come?" Eventually, everyone comes to the same conclusion: Traffic is a function of how many people this retailer reaches and how often — on average — they make a trip to the store. If this retailer reaches 100 customers who frequent the store once a month, traffic is 1,200 customers.

$$\text{Traffic} = f\left(\text{Number of People (\#)} \times \text{Frequency of Visits}\right)$$

What about the average transaction size? Because of point of sale computers, this number is precisely available. The average transaction size is a calculation executed by multiplying the average number of items each time the total button is pushed on the register times the average price per item of all the items in the transaction. Ten items averaging $2 each would mean the average transaction size is $20.

$$\text{Average Transaction Size} = \text{Average Units (\#)} \times \text{Average Price per Unit (\$)}$$

So, making a giant leap in analytical thinking converted into tactical execution, the seller is greeted with the Holy Grail made alive via CPM analysis! In order to generate more revenue (and, thus, lead to more profit), retailers need either more traffic or higher transaction sizes or both.

The seller's role, then, is to stop selling *from* a need (e.g. more facings or a display or expanded item distribution) and start selling *to* a need (more traffic or higher transaction sizes).

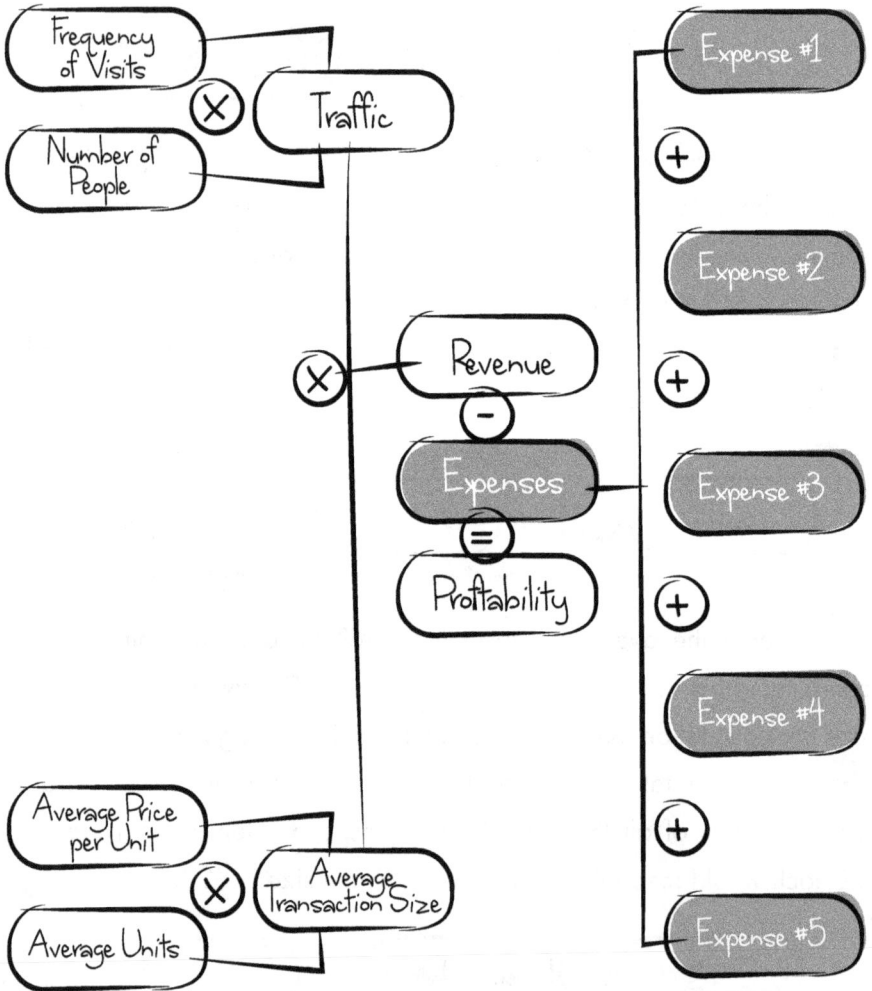

STUN 'em!

When sellers do this, they STUN their customers.

That is, they **Satisfy *Their* Unmet Need**. Of course, here the pronoun "their" refers to the retailer customer, the buyer. When used as the goal in selling, our need is greeted with that dreaded tattoo: "So What?" On the flip side, when used as the goal in selling, their need is greeted by a wonderful and fantastic and energizing jerk of the head and locking of eyes and, well, a look of being STUNned. "Here," the store manager says silently to himself or herself, "is a seller unlike those who come to bother me day after day. Here is someone who speaks my language. Here, finally and at last, is someone who has something to say that is worthy of my ears. Here is someone who is looking at this transaction from my side of the table."

[19

Taking this thought even further (in CPM terms), the buyer thinks: "Here is someone who is not selling me a product or service like all the others. Here is someone who is selling me an idea that, if it works, satisfies my unmet need, my need for traffic or my need for a larger average transaction size. These are needs I cannot deny and cannot dismiss. These are needs seldom if ever mentioned by sellers. I am, truly, STUNned."

That is the premise of this book. STUN your customer to be more successful, to sell more, to sell at a higher price, to sell more quickly, to have FUN as a seller. Having fun is true no matter to whom you sell: A reseller, a consumer, a committee of buyers with mixed points of view; when you are satisfying their unmet needs, it is fun because you're doing a good thing even if you have to drag them along with you a bit. You know exactly what you're doing — and you believe in what you're doing — even if they don't... yet.

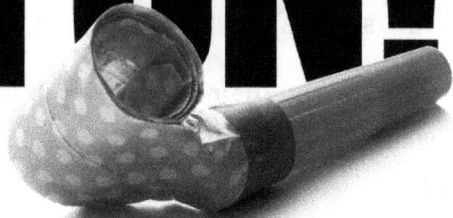

STUN = FUN!

And, as is the case with real selling (which doesn't happen until you hear the word, "No"), STUN gets to be even more fun when customers begin tossing out objections. There are but four types of objections: Misunderstanding, Doubt, Indifference and True Negative. Each type requires a different kind of response. Each type is overcome by STUNning the customer. Each time a seller successfully overcomes an objection, a type of seller's euphoria happens; FUN happens.

When sellers master STUN, the dreaded SAD (Sunday Afternoon Depression) vanishes. SAD sufferers know the feeling: "I have to go to work tomorrow morning. I hate my job. I'm out of control. I'm failing or, at least, not succeeding there."

When sellers master STUN, however, a new vibe happens on Sunday afternoon and it is one of anticipation. You know you are STUNning your customers when you can't wait to see that first buyer on Monday morning and you can't wait for that moment that they see you coming and, rather than scowling at you, they smile at you and ask, "What have you got for me today?" Their arms, rather than folded across their chest, are open. Then, you have STUNned yourself as well.

How Am I Going to Do That?

Businesses are created to STUN.

Without unmet needs, there would be no need for business to exist. So, you might be wondering, how are you going to STUN your customers?

In countless speeches over the years, I introduced myself with the goal of building up my audience rather than myself. I have heard speaker after speaker brag and boast about their achievements, how smart they are and all the wonderful things they have achieved. Me? I said it this way, "I know a whole lot about selling psychology, but you know more about your product and service and customers and competitors than I ever will. True, I did go to college and I did graduate, but I don't remember what I majored in." I always got a laugh and, I think, made a few friends by purposefully not coming off as arrogant, overly smart or better than those to whom I was going to speak.

I told a white lie in that introduction. I really do recall what I majored in. It was "Marketing." I didn't know exactly what marketing was when I decided to major in it. To this day, there are those who can't define it properly. For the most accurate definition, we can go to the Board of Directors of the American Marketing Association who, in July of 2013, approved this definition of the word: "Marketing is the activity, set of institutions, and processes for creating, communicating, delivering and exchanging offerings that have value for customers, clients, partners and society at large."

For purposes of STUN, the phrase upon which I would like to key is "value for customers."

STUN (Satisfy Their Unmet Need) uses customers as the antecedent for the word "their" and "value" is derived from changing what is to what would be better. When you satisfy someone's unmet

[21]

need, you are adding value. And, of course, the word value means that you ought to be paid for it.

The marketing department of every company I have ever worked for, either as an employee, contractor or vendor, has one thing above all else to do: Figure out what their customers' unmet needs are and then create, communicate and deliver products or services to satisfy those needs.

For the sales department and the sales people, the job is different. It is to drill down within customer subsets and clearly define the unmet need for that one particular customer who now sits across the table, choosing product and/or service offerings that will meet that need, clearly communicating the match between the unmet need and the benefits the product or service will deliver and then, most importantly, close the deal. The most major of differences between marketing and sales is the latter point: Sales people, unlike marketing people, must close.

There is another difference. Macromarketing is what most marketing departments do. They study the customer base as a whole. Micromarketing is what sellers must do. They determine the unmet need of the individual customer.

To do this, sellers must resist the notion of taking control of customer conversations. Instead, sellers must commence a conversation and then cede control to the customer so that a clear picture of that individual's unmet need can be fully realized.

That is best done by following a simple process which makes use of cascading open questions.

Open questions are those designed and intended to solicit long and detailed responses. A question that yields a "Yes," or "No," or "Maybe," was, by definition, a closed question.

If the question begins with the words "Do," "Did," "Does" or similar words it will normally yield a one word reply. "Do you like what you see?" "Yes." "Does that meet your need?" "No."

If the question begins with the words "What," "How," or "Why" or similar words, it will normally yield a multi-word reply. "What have you tried in the past?" "How did that work for you?" "Why do you think that is?" These questions cannot be answered with a simple "Yes" or "No."

That means that, to determine the unmet need of the customer sitting across the table, the smart seller asks a lot of open questions beginning with "What," "How," or "Why" or similar words and then becomes silent so as to fulfill the role of listener.

All the things the Marketing Department decided were true are still true, but they are honed, refined and made more specific through this process. Then, all the benefits that the Marketing Department's features deliver can be sorted through and whittled down so that only the ones that clearly STUN this particular buyer are discussed. Instead of taking a "brochure" approach which is almost always overselling since it contains something for everybody, as a savvy seller, we seek to understand our particular customer's needs because we're not talking to everybody. We're talking to this one individual somebody and our mission is to hear and confirm the real, exact and unambiguous unmet need that, if it can be satisfied by us, will lead to value being added and an invoice for products or services being gladly paid.

When I was advising sellers for Pepsi-Cola, Anheuser-Busch, Dr Pepper Snapple, Sara Lee, Dolly Madison, Pennzoil, Dean Foods, Muscle Milk and others who sold to retailers, I almost always studied their customers to determine whether or not it was traffic or transaction size that was their most urgent unmet need. In virtually every case, those customers (Walmart, Target, Ralph's, Applebee's, Kroger, etc.) would tell us that their primary unmet need was a lower price. But, if we STUNned them with a lower price, then our competition would follow us with a still lower price and, after a while, there was no profit to be earned. My job, and the thing I taught over and over again, was that while each of these customers needed a lower price, the more important need was for a product that would either draw traffic (new or repeat or larger party size) or increase transaction size (price per item or items per shopper) or both. Lower prices addressed the issue of lower expenses but traffic and transaction size strategies addressed the issue of revenue. I always prefer to sell revenue because it is more difficult for my competition to "me-too" me and it earns greater profitability for me as the seller.

When I was advising sellers of services — and I admittedly have less experience here — the formula was a bit different. Sellers of services are not selling, as my earlier examples did, to resellers. They are selling to consumers. Consumers don't care about traffic or transaction size. They care about themselves. They are not more selfish about their unmet needs; they just have different unmet needs the seller must address.

At Vance Publishing, the product was advertising. Advertisers needed to draw new customers. At UBS and MasterCard International, the product was financial services. Their customers needed ease and security of payment processing or financial security in retirement or return on current investment dollars and, most of all, trust.

At Helzberg Diamonds, the customer's unmet need is a tangible way to say to another, "I love you." At Dick's Sporting Goods, the customer's unmet need is to escape blisters when breaking in a new pair of running shoes. For Chambers of Commerce, the customer's need is always ill-defined and that may be the main reason I always failed in that channel of business; I couldn't seem to help Chambers satisfy the unmet needs of their membership since they apparently don't know or care what those unmet needs truly are.

For you as a seller, the key is to:

1. Assume what the universe of customers that your corporate marketing department has identified embraces as unmet needs and then...

2. Through the process of asking targeted open questions and careful listening, validate the accuracy of what you heard through the process of asking closed "Nod" questions and

3. Whittle down that universe to a solar system and then a star and then a planet that you can target. STUN the planet, not the universe. Universes are for marketers. Stars? That's for you; both to address and to become.

As a seller myself, my aim is to STUN you with this book. Your unmet need is probably to sell more or to sell for a higher price. This writing is designed by me for sellers so that I might Satisfy Their Unmet Need to sell more or sell for a higher price. If that is you, get ready to find in these pages a new way of thinking about buyers which will lead you to better Sunday afternoons.

WHAT I WOULD HAVE DONE DIFFERENTLY
IF I KNEW THEN WHAT I KNOW NOW

I would do everything differently. When my selling career began in the early 1970's, I did everything wrong. Everything. I will outline for you, Tool by Tool, what I mean.

WHAT YOU SHOULD DO RIGHT NOW

Prepare to think differently about this most honorable of professions: Sales.

SECTION TWO

How to Put **STUN** to Work for You: The **STUN** Toolkit

As you know by now, this book is all about a selling process I call "STUN." For a time, I thought about creating a flow chart for illustrating how to STUN people. There is one problem, however: STUN is not linear in nature. The chart that I would draw would be more complex than the New York City subway map overlaid with a Google map of the Venice canal system.

Rather than a linear process, STUN is a collection of 15 Tools. Much as a mechanic might, you, as the seller, will find yourself confronting a particular situation. You will, from recognition of that situation, choose which Tool or Tools to pull from your Toolbox. In this book, I will describe each Tool in great detail and position it so you know when it is the best choice to achieve your desired end result. At first, you may have to stop and consider your situation before choosing the correct Tool. If you practice the process you will find that your Tool selection will become instinctive, fast and, ultimately, highly effective.

The **STUN**™ Toolkit

The concept, Satisfy Their Unmet Need, has served my customers and me very well over the past few years of my selling life. I only wish I had discovered this Toolkit long ago. Please, go STUN people.

Tool #1	Determining Customer Needs
Tool #2	Speaking "Customer"
Tool #3	The QuickSell®
Tool #4	Turning Features Into Benefits
Tool #5	Selling to Different Personality Types
	■ Selling to Dominant Personalities
	■ Selling to Influencer Personalities
	■ Selling to Steady Personalities
	■ Selling to Compliant Personalities
Tool #6	Selling to Different Customer Roles
Tool #7	Closing the Sale
Tool #8	Overcoming Objections
	■ Objections: Misunderstanding
	■ Objections: Doubt
	■ Objections: Indifference
	■ Objections: True Negative
Tool #9	Handling Tough Customers
Tool #10	Defeating Stalls
Tool #11	No, But, If™
Tool #12	When to Shut Up
Tool #13	Selling in New Products
Tool #14	Smile
Tool #15	Customer Service Later

TOOL # 1

Determining Customer Needs

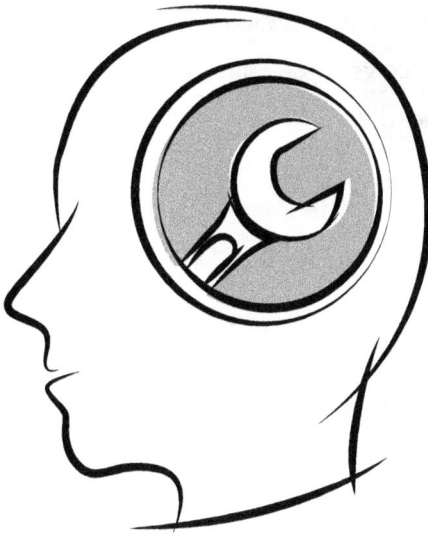

Here's What You're Going to Learn

"Without a Need, Don't Proceed."

If there is one thing that I have said over and over without change during all these many years of working with companies and individual sellers, this is it. If, as an ethical seller, your customer doesn't need what you're selling, you're out of luck; you won't sell anything. If your customer needs what you're selling, you're going to win... and so is your customer. But, you have to do everything right.

THE POINT

Talk less about what you're selling. Talk more about how your customer needs what you're selling and how what you're selling meets or satisfies his need. Remember: Your customer will only buy the solution you are selling because he receives a benefit... and, that only works if the benefit satisfies his unmet need!

My first real sales job was as the Denver-based representative of the Josten's/American Yearbook Company. As I alluded to in Section One, I did everything wrong.

Sure, I won the national award in my first year for most new business signed by a new salesman (there were no female sales representatives then so the gender choice in using "salesman" here, while not inclusive is, in this case, accurate). My sales manager, Tom Jenz, took me aside as I returned from the stage clutching my award and said that I shouldn't think that winning this honor would keep me from getting fired.

"Fired?" I said, shocked.

"Yes, indeed," he said. "If you don't improve your account retention rate next year I'll fire you. You cannot grow your business if all you do is sign new customers. You also have to re-sign your existing business."

His point was lost on me at the time. But I came to see that he was right. You don't gain if you don't retain. I wasn't very good at that. Looking back, I'm not really sure how I signed all that new business either. Perhaps because I was a fresh face and the people I called upon — high school principals and yearbook advisors — were dissatisfied with their current arrangement and were ready to try anything new that might be better than what they already had. I think that, maybe, I was successful with new business by default.

I sold publishing services. If you had asked me what my customers needed, I would have responded by saying, "They need somebody to publish their school yearbook." And, while that is true, it is naïve and superficial.

What they really needed — I now see perfectly in hindsight — was a school yearbook delivered on time and on or under budget. They needed it to contain nothing that would embarrass the school. They needed the kids who served on the yearbook staff to get training in photography, writing and reporting, editing and more.

Had I simply sold "on time and on budget, not embarrassing, educational" instead of "publishing" I would have not only won the trophy for new business, I would have re-signed every customer my predecessor had turned over to me whether they were happy with him or not.

[31

I was selling to the wrong need. No wonder I was only partially successful.

Aside from Josten's, my first real foray into sales training was in July of 1985 with the Pepsi-Cola Bottler's Association in Johnstown, PA. As a contractor, I was hired to help turn former truck drivers into sales professionals. I taught a sales process that was called P.R.O.F.I.T.S. The acronym stood for:

P. Prepare
R. Relate
O. Open the Presentation
F. Feature the Benefits
I. Interact with the Customer
T. Tackle Objections
S. Seal the Deal

In the Prepare section, we talked about determining the customer's need. It was during this time that my thinking began to evolve on this topic, but it was not until much later that I became fanatical about STUN.

Our problem was this: We were selling Pepsi-Cola products. We believed the customer's need was good service, full shelves, rotated product and other "Pepsi-Centric" issues. As I grew into my trainer's role by spending more and more time with the retailers who sold Pepsi to consumers, I learned that we at Pepsi had not drilled deeply enough. What those retailers needed was more profound. They needed more revenue. They achieved that by drawing more store traffic. They achieved that by motivating larger average basket rings from that traffic. Sure, they needed all that other stuff, too, but they needed it less.

At Pennzoil, I was privileged to provide sales training services. All those auto parts dealers needed, I was told by Pennzoil people, was a display of Pennzoil on a front end cap in their stores. I discovered what they really needed was more revenue through increases in traffic and transaction size, just like Pepsi's grocery stores did.

At Anheuser-Busch, again, I was privileged to provide sales training. There, I was told, bar owners needed to add Michelob to their draft beer lineup. Again, that wasn't what they needed. They needed the same things those auto parts dealers and grocery stores needed.

At Interstate Brands Corporation (Dolly Madison Cakes), at Sara Lee, at MasterCard International, Perot Systems, Ace Hardware, Macklanburg-Duncan, Vance Publishing Corporation, Sanofi Animal Health, Simmons Industries and even the Montana State Lottery, the story was the same. In most, if not all, cases, we were selling to the wrong need. In some cases we were close but in other cases we were so far away from what would be truly motivational to the buyer that, in hindsight, I cringe.

Truth be told, what we were doing at all those enterprises wasn't wrong but it wasn't truly right either.

What we didn't do well enough — and the fault is one that I take full responsibility in sharing — was to drill down into the prospects' business models and find the unassailable, undeniable unmet needs and then find ways for our products and services to satisfy those needs.

A Pepsi display promotes impulse purchases which drives up the average basket ring. Now, to be sure, that display has to be full (except for a starter gap) with fully rotated fresh product with themed point-of-sale material, a price card, base wrap, a pole sign and be in a good location. But they didn't need me to sell them all of those things; they were expected. What they needed me to sell to them was the impulse sale that drove up the basket size. Their "sales fatigue" turns into real interest when I talk about STUN: Satisfying Their Unmet Needs. They're never bored when you STUN them.

Michelob on tap raised the average transaction size because a glass of Michelob sold for slightly more than a glass of Miller or Coors or — and we didn't mention this — Bud. Sell the average transaction size; not the Michelob.

Selling lottery tickets increased convenience store traffic for Montana retailers so they could sell them something else besides the ticket to riches. Sell the traffic, not the tickets.

Hostess "shells" promoted the sale of strawberries and Reddi Whip driving up the number of items shoppers purchased which meant, you guessed it, higher basket rings. Sell the extra items, not the shells.

Selling twelve-packs of Bud Light instead of "suitcases" (24 packs) promoted more repeat traffic more quickly. Sell the repeat traffic, not the twelve-packs.

At the Helzberg Diamonds chain of stores, increasing the add-on rate (the number of consumers who bought a full priced item to go along with the promoted sale priced item that drew them into the store) increased store profits. Make sure the selling skills training is about the extra item rather than the discounted item alone.

And, at Nicolet High School in Glendale, WI, where Ms. Dierdra Gonia was the yearbook advisor and my customer, delivering the high school annual on time and without any smart aleck kid making a googly facial expression in the second row of a club photo meant that she slept better at night and had a principal who was anxious to renew her contract for one more year. Sell the good night's sleep, not the color end sheets.

This mantra can be repeated by me over and over and over and I will still come up with the same punch line. Your customers don't need what you need. They don't even need what you're selling. They need what they need. They need what the thing you're selling ultimately does for them. If they are a for-profit enterprise, they need to make more money. But, how do they do that? This is where you will find their true unmet need.

For the vast majority of the people my sales training "students" sold to, the answer was simple: More traffic and a larger transaction size.

At Vance Publishing, however, their trade magazines and newspapers couldn't increase traffic or transaction size for the average reader of Modern Jeweler Magazine. But what the magazine could do was offer up its readers ideas that would help them sell more items or more expensive items to the jewelry shoppers who frequented those stores. But, my "client" at Modern Jeweler was the sales person who sold the ad to the diamond fashion merchant who might purchase a half page ad contract in the book. What did that merchant need? That was how we could sell more ads. If the ad pitched the store on how effective that manufacturer's product was at delivering a full margin extra item to every sale, the readers of the magazine would be highly motivated to buy from that manufacturer and that manufacturer would be highly motivated to buy another ad from Modern Jeweler.

At Macklanburg-Duncan, they made high quality home improvement consumables such as weather stripping and caulk. They sold to hardware retailers in the hardware store and home center channels. They weren't selling to the unmet need of eliminating drafts in window panes. That's what the products actually did, but Lowe's didn't have drafty windows. Lowe's needed—you guessed it—a shopper to buy one more or two more items when they were in the store and caulk was a perfect way to do that. Yes, ultimately, the product had to stop drafts but, in that moment, what it really had to do was fill up shopping carts.

Chevrolet doesn't sell cars and trucks. Chevrolet sells vehicles that make drivers and passengers feel special and safe.

Southwest Airlines doesn't sell tickets. It sells painless arrival at a vacation or business destination.

Samsung doesn't sell phones. It sells, well, it sells "cool." "Can you hear me now?" (from Verizon) is the price of entry; it isn't the thing that truly turns people's heads.

What is your customer's unmet need? Be careful here. Don't tell me what your unmet need is. Don't tell me that they need to buy some of your widgets. They don't buy your widgets to buy your widgets. They buy your widgets to make their profit and loss statement stronger. They buy them because your widgets make their business better. This distinction is critical.

Buyers don't care about what you need. They care about what they need. If you sell to your need, you will ultimately fail. If you sell to theirs, you will win this year, next year and forever.

STUN your customers and they will love you for it. You can only STUN them if you precisely define and then satisfy their unmet need.

[35

WHAT I WOULD HAVE DONE DIFFERENTLY
IF I KNEW THEN WHAT I KNOW NOW

At the Josten's/American Yearbook Company, I would only have spoken of paper quality, foil stamped covers or gang separation of color photographs if they forced me. Instead of talking about product features, that is, the things important to me, I would have talked about educating kids, delivering on time and on budget and making sure nothing embarrassing slipped into the pages of their yearbook. Oh, man; I would have been great.

WHAT YOU SHOULD DO RIGHT NOW

Analyze your customer's business. What truly motivates them every day? Is it profitability? If so, how do they make a profit? Oh, one more thing; you can help them make a larger profit by cutting your prices. Don't do it. Your competitor will eventually match you and you'll be back to square one. Instead, figure out how you can help them generate more revenue. That has always—always—worked wonders for me.

[37

Confirm your understanding of this concept. Watch our ej4 video, "Determining Customer Needs," at STUNselling.com/customer_needs.

38]

TOOL #2

Speaking "Customer"

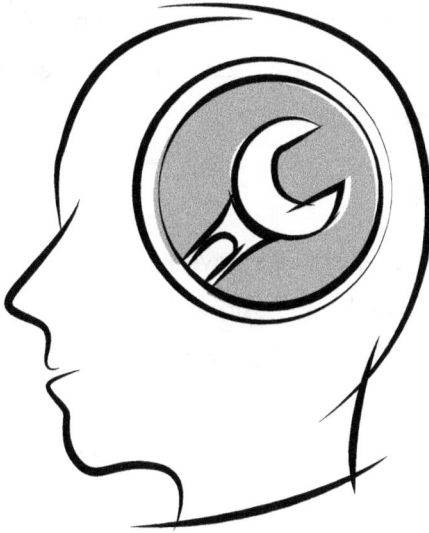

Here's What You're Going to Learn

People are more receptive to sellers who **"speak their language"** by referring to terms and conditions of the sale using vocabulary familiar and customary to them.

THE POINT

Don't talk your talk; talk their talk. Customers appreciate sellers who speak their language. These customers will tell sellers about their problems, what they need, what makes them happy and what is really important to them. They get snippy with salespeople who don't speak their language — in fact, these customers turn up their noses at ignorant sellers, often steering them wrong and treating them as if they are not worthy of the customer's time.

Let's face it, as sellers, customers have the ability to frustrate us and, I suppose, we have the ability to frustrate them in return. One unassailable truth of selling is that frustrated buyers are slow to buy and frustrated sellers are ineffective.

What are the keys to avoiding frustration on both sides of the sale? There are many, but chief among them is a very basic, and often overlooked, tenet: Buyers and sellers must speak the same language.

Many years ago, I made my first trip to France. I didn't enjoy the trip nearly as much as I might have because I found the French people I met to be amazingly standoffish, unfriendly and even arrogant. This is likely to come as no surprise to you because, stereotypically speaking, the French have long held this negative reputation. At a restaurant, for example, I would clearly and slowly explain (in English) what I wanted to order, but I became frustrated because they did not understand me. It amazed me that the restaurants in France — in Paris and throughout the countryside — did not insist that all their servers speak the English language. Here I was, ready to spend my hard earned U.S. dollars in their establishments and they did not go to the trouble to learn my language. Frankly, I didn't enjoy France because I certainly didn't enjoy the French people who didn't speak English.

[41]

Each day of my trip, I felt my demeanor worsen. As I expected poor treatment, I became more defensive whenever I would enter a bakery or coffee shop or restaurant. I got what I expected; in fact, with each passing day, service levels seemed to fall. Bottom line, as my attitude declined, the people with whom I came in contact never failed to match my negativity with increasing rudeness.

I vowed to never return.

A couple of years later, at the invitation of a good friend, Yvonne, I hesitantly returned to France. Yvonne explained to me that my initial impression of the French people was incorrect. She explained that they are a warm and welcoming people who have a high desire to please visitors. At her behest and urging, I worked to set aside my first impression and go with an open mind. On this second visit, I was amazed at how much the French people had changed. My experience was exactly the opposite of my first trip. With Yvonne guiding me through France, speaking (in French) on my behalf, everywhere we went, we were welcomed.

My only frustration was that I didn't understand what my friend was saying to the various people we encountered. As she spoke, I struggled to catch a word here and there that I understood but they spoke so quickly that I had little success. But, as Yvonne and those with whom we came into contact bantered back and forth, their smiles were contagious. I found myself smiling right along with them even though I was in the dark as to what they were saying.

What a wonderful trip it turned out to be.

The difference was not, of course, in the passing of time nor was it due to visiting different people or different places and, no, there had not been some major countrywide cultural shift. The difference, as you have already discerned, was that my host spoke fluent French. She spoke their language. Because there was no language barrier, there was no personal barrier. Because no barriers existed, relationships — even fleetingly — flourished.

You have already gotten my point. If you want to feel welcomed in France (and, really, any other country you visit, for that matter), learn to speak French (or whatever is the common language of the country in question). Even if you don't speak the language, if you are with someone who does, you will earn an entirely better experience.

The same is true with customers. Buyers think like buyers and they speak buyer; not seller. And, of course, they speak the language of their industry, of their company and of their perspective.

For example, when I worked with Pepsi-Cola Bottlers sales teams and called on large format retailers — known to you and me as grocers — I heard the customers speak of their customers' (known as shoppers) "baskets." Wondering what that meant, I asked. The shoppers' baskets were described in terms of dollar amounts. The average shopper's basket in one store might be $21.

One day later, when I worked with Pepsi's on-premise sales teams (the ones who called on restaurants), I heard the customers speak of their customers' (known as diners or eaters) "check." Wondering what that meant, I asked. The diners' checks were also described in terms of dollar amounts. The average diner's check in one account might be $21.

The point here is a simple one. When Pepsi would transfer one of their sellers from the grocery channel to the restaurant channel, that person had to quickly stop talking about <u>baskets</u> and start talking about <u>checks</u> even though, from a layman's perspective, the dollar amounts were identical. To do otherwise would be to invite customer reactions that would be amazingly standoffish, unfriendly and even arrogant.

Every customer contact began to remind me of my trips to France. The lesson: When in France, speak French (or defer to a companion or partner who does). When in grocery stores, speak the language of grocery stores and not the language of restaurants.

A few more examples...

In the baking business, I found the sellers spoke about product that remained unsold in stores as "stale." Stale did not refer to bread that had become dry and crusty instead of moist and soft. It meant bread that had remained unsold past its "pull date." Pull date meant the last day that it should remain on sale before being pulled from the shelf.

I thought that "stale" was a bad thing, something that was to be avoided at all costs because it would indicate goods that could not be sold but, instead, had to be destroyed. That would cost my bakery customers money and lots of it.

However, it was quickly explained to me that there was an optimum amount

[43

of "stale" that each route sales person should achieve and that amount was never zero. Zero stale meant that, at some point, the bread shelf in the store was "wiped," meaning completely sold out. That meant, to the bread company, that at least one sale was lost because the person who came looking for that brand found none on the shelf. That meant that, because they needed bread, maybe — just maybe, they bought the competition's bread on this trip. What if they liked the competitor's product? Maybe next time, they switched their allegiance from my client's brand to their competition's brand. That is a disaster which should never be allowed to happen. The shelf was never to be sold down to zero.

Since the bread route sales force was of a limited number, they couldn't be in every store all the time to keep the shelves full. No amount of stock rotation on the shelf—since there was no room for "back stock"—would solve this problem. Management expected the sales force to bring back some bread and that was called "stale." If there was no stale from a particular sales person, management took that to mean that there existed on those routes some unacceptable out-of-stock situations. Stale was good — as long as it wasn't too much. Had I not understood the language of the bakery customer, I would not understand this critical sales tactic.

In the beer business, when Anheuser-Busch adopted the term "Born On Dating" it was designed to replace a code dating system that focused on product freshness that looked at pull dates. Since the "Bud Man" sold more beer than anyone else at that time, "he" was in the store more frequently and, as a result, the Budweiser or Bud Light on the shelf was "fresher" than the Coors or Coors Light that sat next to it. Anheuser-Busch wanted to point out that "fresher" beer was better than "old" beer. As a result, "Born On" was, well, born.

A-B wholesalers pitched this concept to bars and liquor stores and, of course, to beer drinkers. And, to a great extent, they bought it — that is to say they bought the concept and bought the Bud as well. It was a point of difference that was very difficult for the competitor brewers to match and Anheuser-Busch needed to insert it into the language to make it work to their benefit. It met with limited success but every little bit helps when you are battling for single digit increases in market share.

Anheuser-Busch had done this many times before. Three years before I began consulting for Anheuser-Busch, the company executed a move of pure genius — with the help of brilliant work from ad agency D'Arcy McManus & Masius. Most notable was their effort to make up for lost time when Miller Brewing bested them in the lower calorie beer segment known as "light beer." Miller came out with Miller Lite. Miller's brilliance was in positioning the brand — using retired star athletes — as a beer that had "great taste" but was "less filling." That meant you could drink more and not get fat. The idea was to STUN beer drinkers as they got older and rounder. Arguably, the use of the word "Lite" was both brilliant and a strategic error. Due to copyright, Budweiser couldn't use the word "Lite." But, they could use the more familiar "Light," which Miller's legal team said was not a copyrightable word in this context.

[45

Some consumers wanted a light beer so they bellied up to the bar and ordered that. "Give me a light," they might say. Invariably, they were served a "Lite," a Miller Lite.

Bud Light began to run a seemingly unending stream of commercials on this theme: A beer drinker sat at the bar and said, "Gimme a Light." From the side, a flaming arrow would be shot to stick in the wall. The consumer would say, "I meant a Bud Light." Soon Bud Light owned the category. Sure, a key pricing decision made a gigantic impact but the trick was to get the consumer to change his (or her) language. Gimme a Bud Light turned the tables on Lite. Consumers were STUNned but by Bud Light rather than Miller Lite.

And, back to the soft drink business, the Pepsi folks fought—and in some places still fight—an ongoing language war with grocers. The word "Coke" had come to mean any soft drink. I recall being in a Piggly Wiggly supermarket in the South and seeing directory signs saying, simply, "Cokes." You know overhead directory signs in supermarkets? They say, "snacks, health food, bread, etc." Well, for this store's soft drink aisle, the signs said, "Cokes." I decided to try and make a point with the store manager by asking, "Where is the Pepsi?" He told me, "They're right down the Cokes aisle — over there." To make my point, I said, "I don't want Cokes; I want a Pepsi." He told me — and I will never ever forget this—"Oh, we got all kinda Cokes. We got 7-Up Cokes and A&W Cokes and Orange Cokes. We got whatever kinda Cokes you want."

Pepsi-Cola had to get retailers to stop thinking of their soft drink business as "Coke" business. Anheuser-Busch had to get their retailers to stop thinking about their light beer business as "Lite" business.

What about you? Do you need to not only learn to speak your customers' language correctly but also change their language? Speaking their language is easier than changing it to suit your offerings. You can't STUN them if you cannot articulate their unmet need in their language.

I knew a guy who published several books, some using the letters "PhD" after his name. I mention the PhD part for one reason only:

He always — then and now — spoke as one might imagine a PhD would speak. When a one syllable word would suffice, he would substitute a multi-syllable word. When plain talk would perfectly explain a situation, he would substitute multi-syllabic psychobabble. And, if a simple sentence would well serve the purpose, he would write one with scores of words and endless complexity.

That was all fine when he was speaking to someone of his own ilk. His problem was that he was often speaking with clients or potential clients who were plain spoken. His sales efforts were, as a result, only marginally successful. The reason is clear: His former customers describe him now in unflattering terms that stem primarily from his way of speaking his language rather than their language.

My guidance to you: **Be plain spoken**. Use simple sentences wherever you can. If a simple word makes the point, use it rather than a word the listener doesn't recognize or might misunderstand. But, when speaking to someone whose language is one of complexity in both word and structure, match them phrase for phrase if you can. Don't bluff. In France, those who butcher their beautiful language are greeted with contempt.

Speak your customer's language. When in France, speak French. If you don't know French, take someone with you who does. When in the world of insurance, speak insurance. When in the world of banking, speak banking. When in the world of motor oil, speak motor oil. If you don't speak insurance, banking or motor oil, find someone who does speak that language to go with you and let them take the lead.

[47

WHAT I WOULD HAVE DONE DIFFERENTLY
IF I KNEW THEN WHAT I KNOW NOW

Listening better means not only hearing what your prospect is saying but also hearing the words they use to make their points. Then, I would have "spoken their language" by using the vocabulary they use — the vocabulary familiar to them.

Over the years, I have learned in restaurants, "covers" means "how many people are in the party" and "average check" means how much each diner spends. In supermarkets, "average transaction size" or "basket ring" means how much each customer spends; they don't measure how many people are in the shopping party except, perhaps, in the dine-in deli department. In the soft drink business where sellers encounter customers from both channels, sellers need to remember to speak supermarket in supermarkets and restaurants in restaurants.

WHAT YOU SHOULD DO RIGHT NOW

Learn and use the vocabulary familiar to and used by your prospect when referring to features, benefits, terms and conditions. Set your words aside and use theirs instead. That means you must become a great listener hearing not only what they say but what words they use to say it.

Watch the companion ej4 video, "Speaking Customer," located at STUNselling.com/speaking_customer to solidify your understanding of this important concept.

[49

50]

TOOL #3

The QuickSell®

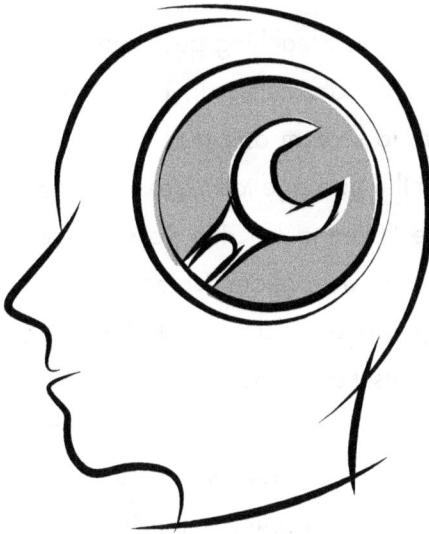

Here's What You're Going to Learn

To Get:	Your customers to buy more quickly
You Should:	**Employ the QuickSell Process**
Which Would:	Get you to "Yes" or an objection right away
I Could:	Show you how it works if you'll just read on

THE POINT

Simple sales don't have to take a long time. Using the QuickSell methodology, you can close a sale in as few as five seconds.

For as long as I have been teaching people how to sell, if there is one thing, just one thing, that absolutely drives me crazy, that frustrates me, that makes me want to scream and tear out my hair, that one thing is this: HURRY UP! Cut the garbage talk. Get to the point. ASK for a "Yes."

In the movie "Glengarry Glen Ross," Alec Baldwin delivers a despicably profane and outrageous "sales meeting" speech to a group of mostly failing high pressure salesmen. Baldwin says, "A-B-C. Always Be Closing." He repeats it and repeats it. When I first saw the film, I jolted upright in my seat because Dave Ramberg, the man who first taught me selling skills back in 1972 at Josten's/American Yearbook Company at the Howard Johnson Hotel meeting room in Topeka, Kansas, said the same thing but in a more socially acceptable manner: Always Be Closing.

Always Be Closing

Always Be Closing. Always Be Closing. That was years before Baldwin delivered his tirade on film but — and the point here is critical — whether you are selling high school yearbook publishing services to school principals or semi-worthless real estate to naïve "suckers," or even the blocks to the Pharaoh to build the Great Pyramid, the message is and will continue to be the same: Always Be Closing.

But, I couldn't bring myself to do it. I wasn't a high pressure guy. And, like many before me and many who will follow, I was afraid. As a seller, many dread the "No." Many fear it more than anything. To avoid the "No," they simply don't ask. They just keep selling and selling hoping against hope that the buyer will stop them, let them off the hook and say, "OK. You've sold me. Where do I sign?"

You and I both know that doesn't happen.

So, how do I conform to ABC and not seem high pressure? How do I get to a close quickly, but not seem like one of Baldwin's high-pressure boiler room real estate pitchmen?

It's easy. Just learn the QuickSell process.

Four simple steps that are logical, smart and, maybe most important of all, completely and totally ethical when delivered honestly.

As you will read, these steps are the steps I use to begin every chapter of this book. My intent is to both teach you how to use this process and show you how through active demonstration:

1) To Get: ▶ 2) You Should: ▶ 3) Which Would: ▶ 4) I Could.

"Ms. Owen, to get more people in your store, you should run this package at this price in your ad which would bring people in here from the store across the way and all across town. I could give the ad slick to your marketing folks if you like..."

"Mr. O'Brien, to increase your average check, you should put these table tents on every high top in the place so folks will buy a bucket instead of a single bottle and spend a bunch more money with you. I could put them on the tables for you right now if that's OK..."

"Kyle, <u>to get</u> your renewals up, <u>you should</u> bundle this training with memberships <u>which would</u> keep your existing members on your rolls so you can grow more quickly. <u>I can</u> set up the copy for your website with your webmaster next week if you say the word..."

The 1) **To Get**: part is nothing more than a restatement of their unmet need.

The 2) **You Should**: part is nothing more than what you want them to do.

The 3) **Which Would**: part is the benefit — or positive end result that happens when they do what you want them to do.

The 4) **I Could**: part is a close — what you will do.

There is a very quiet, in fact, a SILENT, fifth step to this process. That is, once you've said, "I could..." finish with "...is that okay?" or "...how does that sound?" Then, be SILENT! Say nothing. Do not derail your sale by letting your customer off the hook! Engage your patience. Wait for the response.

1) "Mitch, to get your add-on metric to rise...

2) "...you should send a nano video to every salesperson on the team on Wednesday...

3) "...which would get them focused on selling one more thing to every customer who buys something for Valentine's Day...

4) "...I could reserve the studio for taping next Tuesday if that fits your schedule." [Be SILENT!]

When you lead with the need, you're taking that critical first step of STUNning your customer. You're getting them focused on what is of paramount importance to them: Their unmet need. Everybody is motivated by getting the thing that meets their unmet need, that thing that turns their unmet need into a met need. Need satisfaction is a primary motivator of all human beings. So, lead with that.

Never lead with what you want them to do. When you lead with what you want them to do, what you want them to buy (e.g. your feature, your idea), you are leading with the weakest thing that you'll talk about all day because you didn't put it in context.

[55

No grocer wants to buy another display. No car owner wants an oil change. No restaurant owner wants to change soft drink suppliers. No sales manager wants to go to the trouble to communicate with all of his or her sales team members.

What the grocer wants is a higher average market basket ring. What the car owner wants is a long and carefree ownership experience with their car. What the restauranteur wants is a consumer who buys a soft drink rather than takes a free cup of water. What the sales manager wants is higher store sales volumes.

Don't sell what you are selling.

Sell what the thing you are selling delivers to the buyer.

But, to make it easier and quicker, put it in context first. Lead with their need. Without that need, don't proceed. The need is the thing about which you both can wholeheartedly agree. When your prospect is agreeing — silently or verbally or with a nod — to your statement of need, he is set up to warmly receive what you're selling IF you quickly cut to the benefit he derives from buying it. Remember, he doesn't want what you're selling. He wants what you're selling does for him in that it satisfies his unmet need.

It makes sense for him to say "Yes." Why wouldn't he? He is in agreement that he has an unmet need. He needs it to be met. That's what happens when he buys what you're selling. But you have to say it the right way and you have to say it right away.

This is not the time to impress your buyer with your fancy vocabulary or with your talent for complex sentence structure. This is the time for brevity, for simplicity, for fewer eloquent words.

When I did sales training classes for Pepsi-Cola, I would have everyone write out on a notepad a sample QuickSell that they could use with one of their customers the next day. We had discussed the unmet needs of their customers whether they were large format grocery stores or small format convenience stores or quick serve restaurants. They certainly knew what they were selling. We had discussed, at length, what benefits would accrue to their customers if they would only buy what was being sold. And they knew what the "I Could" next step ought to be.

I would say, "OK. Write one." And then I would move to the side and take a seat avoiding eye contact with the room and maintaining absolute silence for 30 seconds or so. I broke the silence with these words, "Make it short and sweet."

Then I would wait for a couple of minutes, stand, return to the center of the room and ask for a volunteer. "Please read aloud what you wrote," I would ask. In the flip chart days I would use a marker and in the computer projector days I would use my keyboard on a blank Word document to write that person's words in big letters for all to see.

Then, in the old days, I would ask, "Who has a watch with a second hand?" Later, it was, "Who's got a stopwatch on their phone?" Either way, I would ask the author of this particular QuickSell to read it aloud. Typically, it would be somewhere in the vicinity of a 30-second speech.

Then, I would ask, "Let's all find words to remove from this pitch to make it shorter but still make the QuickSell points. Who has an idea?" Then, I would wait. With a red marker or by using Word's Comment feature, as a group, we would edit.

Someone would come up with one idea for the To Get part. Someone else would reword the Which Would. Another person might shorten the I Could. When we were finished, we had essentially the same QuickSell but it was shorter. Ten seconds was wonderful. Fifteen was good. More than fifteen? Too long. "This isn't rocket science we're doing here," I would say, "This is simple. And, it must be quick."

Then, I would pair up the participants and have them edit each other's scripts for length. The end result was succinct with no wasted words and no unnecessary embellishment. Almost without exception, what we came up with was powerful and it made sense and it was put in context and it set up the buyer to say the word we all want to hear. "Yes."

Oh, what a lovely word "Yes" is! It is up to you to get them to feel good about saying it.

QuickSell will get you sales more quickly, more powerfully and more logically. Now it's up to you to ask for the sale. Be quick about it!

WHAT I WOULD HAVE DONE DIFFERENTLY
IF I KNEW THEN WHAT I KNOW NOW

Dave Ramberg had a nickname for me back in the mid-70's when I was Milwaukee-based as one of his American Yearbook Company sales team. He called me, "Sweaty Hand Red." My hair was red in those days rather than the grey that people tell me it is now. The sweaty hands came because I was nervous. I was afraid to ask for the order. I was not executing my A-B-C's: Always Be Closing. I was scared. I feared "No." My palms would perspire.

If I had the QuickSell then, my confidence would have soared. My palms would have had no reason to sweat. I would have had a process, a formula, a step-by-step way to get from what I knew those principal's wanted to what I wanted those principal's to do. If only I had known.

WHAT YOU SHOULD DO RIGHT NOW

Write a few QuickSell "scripts" that fit your customers and your product or service with your benefits and what you want them to do. Write them down. Then, edit. The fewer words you have in your final version, the quicker your QuickSell will be. Aim for 10 seconds.

Brush up on your understanding of the QuickSell process. Visit STUNselling.com/quicksell to watch a short ej4 video summarizing this important concept.

[59

60]

TOOL #4

Turning Features Into Benefits

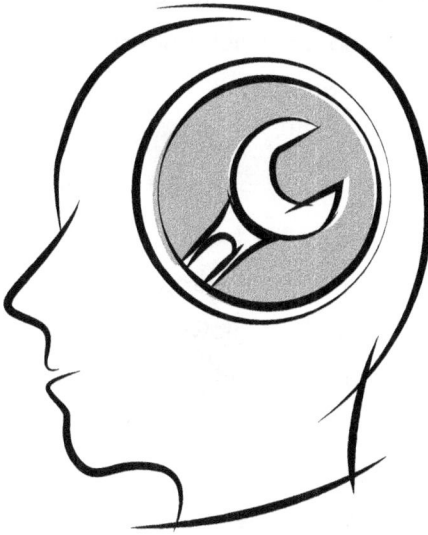

Here's What You're Going to Learn

Translating features into benefits is the first skill a successful seller must master.

However, most training at many companies is actually product-focused (i.e. feature-focused) training, rather than benefit-focused training. The sales force is taught what the product is, has or does. Experts from all over the company show pictures of products, product details, innovations, colors, sizes, pricing, packaging and more. All of that is important. More important, however, are the benefits all of those product or service features deliver to the prospective customer. Without the benefits, the buyer won't buy.

THE POINT

Features are boring. Benefits are enticing, motivational and the reason people buy. Talking on and on about product or service features will kill a sale. Talking succinctly about benefits — if they satisfy an unmet need — leads to a faster and better sale.

The "Circle of Sales," when executed properly, will lead the buyer to think of the seller as a partner. To do so, however, it is important to understand the customer's unmet need. The script goes something like this...

- "You need this...
- "I've got this...
- "Which will do this...
- "This will satisfy your unmet need!"

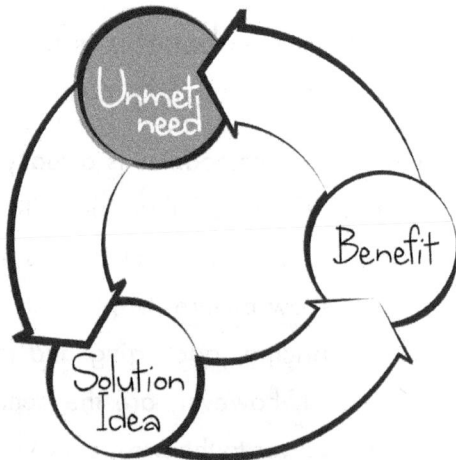

In the past, when delivering sales training classes, I used a pair of big flip charts on easels and markers in four colors to make my points. Several of the diagrams I used to routinely draw still pop into my head fairly regularly. None more so than "The Staircase".

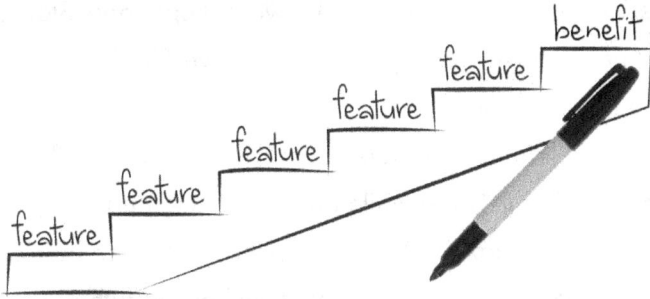

I would draw, well, a one dimensional staircase in black marker and I'd label the bottom riser with the word "feature". A feature is what a product or service is, has or does. The Dell laptop I am currently writing on is an old Latitude E6410. I am running Windows 7 on this machine. I am using Microsoft Word as my word processing software. This machine has an intel Core i5 vPro processor "inside". Each and every one of these points of information is a feature and each and every one of these points is boring.

I know they are boring to you because, and I'll bet money this is true, you are asking yourself "So What?" "What do I care?" "What difference does it make?" "What's in it for me?"

Here's an example: Here I sit writing this book on my laptop. Say I ask myself, "So What?" after I write down "laptop" as a feature on the bottom rung of that staircase, I get started on going to a new place.

[63

Laptop. So What? A laptop is portable. I write "portable" on the second rung of the staircase.

Portable. So What? Portable means that I can pick it up and take it with me to Starbucks (I did a good bit of sales training for the North American Coffee Partnership between Pepsi and Starbucks) or aboard my next Southwest flight to Dallas Love Field. I write "take it with me" on the third rung.

Take it to Starbucks or aboard Southwest. So What? I can write while I relax. I scribble "write while I relax" on the fourth rung.

Write while I relax. So What? I get the book done painlessly and in less time. I write "painless and in less time" on the fifth rung.

It's finished. So What? Well, about this time, it occurs to me that the "So What?" question is no longer needed. My unmet need was to "finish the book." That's the top rung of this staircase.

What that means is that the benefit to me of the laptop computer is a painlessly and quickly completed book. *Voilà!* The computer manufacturer needs to sell me that because that's my unmet need. I don't understand nor do I care about its piece parts or how it was made. I care about the finishing of my book.

The feature or features are boring. The benefit is exhilarating. The benefit is exciting. The benefit is what I'm after while the feature is just a means to an end.

Once I had the staircase drawn, I would ask the assembled group if all those features were so boring why don't I just completely skip over them? For some products or services, you could do that. You could say, "Buying this laptop will help you painlessly and quickly finish your book." That's STUNs me and I'll buy. But, with a display of Mountain Dew 12-pack cans, you couldn't just say, "A display of Mountain Dew will make your store more profitable." You had to walk the customer up the staircase; you cannot pole vault from the bottom feature to the top benefit. Take the stairs — make it clean.

You'd say, "A display of properly merchandised Mountain Dew 12-packs on a front end cap will grab your shoppers' attention, they'll pick up one — or maybe even two — and put them in their basket. As they complete their circuit, if they walk down the salty snack aisle, they'll subconsciously think about a bag of Guy's Chips (never heard of them? Well, I used to do training videos for them many years ago) to go along with the Dew. When they get to the register, they've got two extra items in the basket driving up the transaction size. And, as a bonus, since the chips weren't on sale, they are a full margin item to boot. So, in that way, a display of Mountain Dew will make your store more profitable." And, believe it or not, it's true and honest and ethical and factual... and it works! The store manager nods. You close. B-I-N-G-O!

When I worked for what was called The Owners Institute at Ace Hardware, I would tell a story that helps to further illustrate this point.

I would stand at a display of gas string trimmers; you know, those things that you use in your yard to trim the edge of your sidewalk or fence. If a store associate came by, that was good. If they asked if they could help me, that was even better. I would ask, "Tell me, please, how these string trimmers work. You have one for $79.99, another one for $99.99 and another one for $199.99. Why is this one (for $199.99) worth one and a half times more than that one (for $79.99)?"

The answer I would get would often be, "Well that one for $199.99 is better." Genius!

"Yeah, I get that," I said. "But why? What makes it worth one-hundred-and-twenty-bucks more than this other one?"

Invariably, the associate would lean in and start reading me the bullet points from the package. This one's got a quick-connect split-boom straight shaft and a 30CC 2-cycle engine. It cuts a 17" swath and has a heavy duty automatic clutch and even comes with an eight inch weed blade."

"OK," I would say. "So..."

"Oh, well this one which costs less has a curved shaft and a 25CC 2-cycle engine with at 15" swath. Oh, it also has a 0.95 fixed dual line head and, oh, look at this: a clear fuel tank."

Oh, boy. I'm excited now. Not.

What he should have said is simple: "This one is worth $120 more if you want to finish the trimming job faster and with less physical effort. If not, buy the less expensive one." The message is that the benefit to me is quicker and easier. The price for that is $120 more. I don't know a 25CC engine from a 30CC engine and I'll bet I'm not alone. To say that one is more powerful than the other is to call me stupid. I don't care to be called stupid. If I ask, just tell me that "the 30CC is a more powerful engine which means that you'll get the job done more quickly. If that's what you want to do, spend the money."

I would write all those features on the staircase diagram. Then I would connect the risers with the words: Which Means.

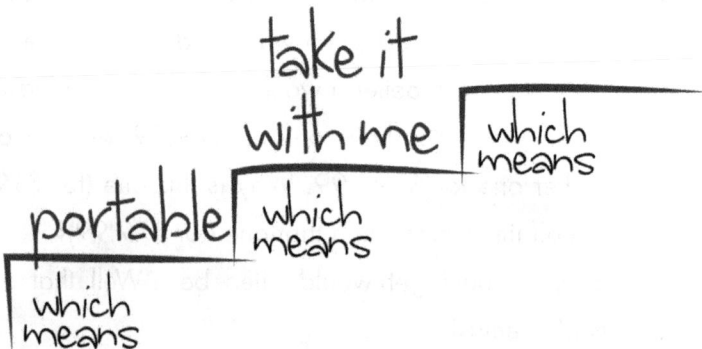

This one has a 30CC engine **which means** that it is more powerful **which means** that you'll get the trimming job done more quickly with less effort and you won't be as tired when you're done.

You won't be as tired when you're done? That's the benefit statement. It's motivational to me. It's motivational to me because that's my unmet need: To get the trimming done and not be worn out when I'm finished.

Don't pole vault from the bottom riser to the top or your logic may be lost on the buyer. Tell them about the steps in between using "**which means**" to get you from one riser to the next.

[67

You'll know when you get to the top. How? The facial expression of the customer will change from bored or confused to one of recognition. You might even get a nod. If you get that facial change or nod, close. "Would you like me to carry it up to the register for you?" Then, shut up.

People don't buy features. They buy what those features mean to them; they buy how those features STUN them. So remember to talk much more about benefits than you do features.

There's a catch. A true benefit must satisfy the buyer's unmet need. If it doesn't, it's not a true benefit. If I told you that my main reason for buying a string trimmer is that I am a couch potato and I need to get a workout, don't sell me quicker and easier. Change the benefit. "This 30CC engine is heavier. It will get you the workout you want and the edges that look perfect. Is that what you're looking for?" I'll nod. You'll close.

I love selling.

WHAT I WOULD HAVE DONE DIFFERENTLY
IF I KNEW THEN WHAT I KNOW NOW

At Josten's/American Yearbook Company, I remember that we had a picture cropping tool called a PhotoFit. I talked about how it worked, how it was made of durable plastic and how it would help kids to crop and enlarge or reduce photographs so that they fit on the layout they had drawn for the page. Knowing what I know now, I would have said, "The PhotoFit teaches your kids about geometry and how to constrain proportions. If they are headed for architecture or engineering as a career, this will energize them."

WHAT YOU SHOULD DO RIGHT NOW

Look at your product brochures. Read the bullet points. Ask "So What?" after each bullet point. Keep asking until you find yourself saying, "So that's what it ultimately does. And, that's what you really want, isn't it?" If you can envision your customer nodding his or her head at that point and saying, "Yes," then you're at the top of the staircase. You made it all the way to the benefit. That's your job. STUN them.

[69

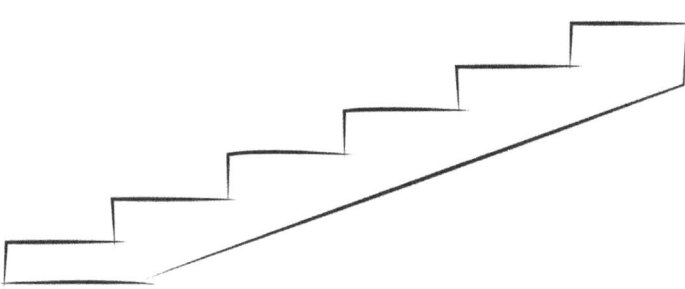

To further your clarity around turning features into benefits, watch the ej4 video at STUNselling.com/features_benefits.

70]

TOOL #5

Selling to Different Personality Types

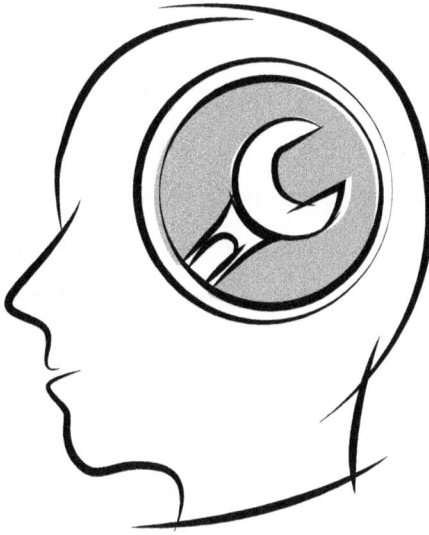

Here's What You're Going to Learn

There are four basic personality types that you must sell to:

Dominant, Influencer, Steady and Compliant

Your best chance of closing a sale is to recognize the personality type of your buyer and sell to him/her based on the way in which he/she prefers to interact with others.

THE POINT

When it comes to closing the sale, your personality type as a seller is irrelevant. Instead, focus on your customer — identify his/her primary personality type and sell to that style. You will achieve startlingly superior results.

For a time during my tenure at Josten's, I held the role of National Sales Recruiter for the company's yearbook publishing division. Management of the company believed strongly in a screening tool then called the Performax Personality Profile System. As a part of my job, I administered this instrument to dozens of candidates for sales positions at the company.

Years later, when I applied for a seminar leader position with Padgett Thompson, I again ran into this tool. It was a key element of their leading money maker, a seminar entitled "Basic Supervision." I delivered over 800 seminars at PT and about half of them used this instrument as a part of the experience. A bit of quick arithmetic tells me that I administered this tool to approximately 30,000 people while leading those seminars. It was so well received by workshop participants that I later used the instrument with audiences at Pepsi-Cola, Anheuser-Busch, Pennzoil, Dolly Madison Bakeries, Ace Hardware and many more. It delivers uncanny insights.

Based upon the book *The Emotions of Normal People*, written in 1928 by William Moulton Marston, the premise of the personality profile is that all "normal" people have in their personalities four tendencies — you may have, at some point in your career, heard this concept referred to as DISC, namely:

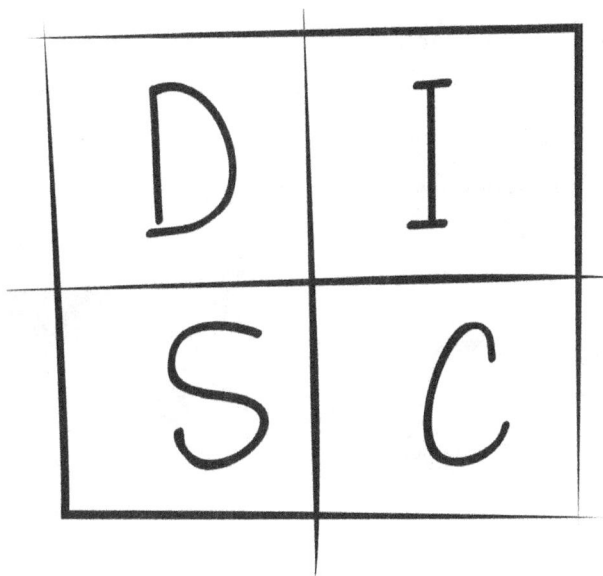

D   for dominance

I   for influencing or inducement

S   for sanguine or steady or submission

C   for compliance or completeness

[As an aside, just for fun, look up Marston on the internet and you'll learn that as a comic book author, he also created Wonder Woman.]

The Personality Profile System is, in actuality, a behavioral assessment tool which, using labels for the four personality types, predicts how a dominant — or "High D" — person might react in a situation and how that reaction is different from how a "High I" or "High S" or "High C" person might react.

As a seller, I became intrigued with the idea that my personality — I am a High D, High I blend — might work well or poorly based on my ability and willingness to adjust my approach to the personality of my prospect. Said another way, I wanted to see if my natural approach worked well on all four types of prospects. It turned out that I got better results when I modified my own behavior to ignore my natural tendencies and, instead, assumed a different approach based upon the personality of the person to whom I was selling. In actuality, my results were startlingly better when I better accommodated the buyer's personality. Simply put, since I couldn't change them, I had to change myself.

Here's what you can expect from each of Marston's personality types:

- **D — Dominant**.

  Dominant types want you to get to the point, close quickly, have short answers to objections and avoid jargon and technical minutiae. With dominant buyers, tell them the end of the story first. Dominant buyers require a unique approach and, in fact, dominant sellers most often win with dominant buyers. If you're not a dominant seller then you need to wear your "dominant mask" when selling to these buyers. Don't worry, you can take it off when you leave — but not before.

- **I — Influencer**.

  Influencers really like people — they will like you and you will probably like them in return. The problem is that they like your competitor just as much as they like you. They don't want to hurt anybody's feelings and they would love to find a way to make everybody happy. In the process of them making your competitor happy they are going to make you sad. Handling them means more than just befriending them. Make no mistake: These buyers are not easy. You must deal with them in a way that makes them see you as their friend. However, you can never speak ill of your competition or your competitions' offerings because you will turn influencers off by doing so. You must always be positive. Never criticize your competition; instead, get them to do it. Don't complain; for them, life is good and they'll like you more if you agree with that outlook. They like to buy from people they like.

■ **S — Steady**.

Steady personalities don't like change. If you're the incumbent, that's great. If your competition is the incumbent, it's not. While dominant persons may say, "Let's do something even if it's wrong," your steady customers will say, "Let's do nothing unless it's right." The key for you when selling to steady prospects is to show that the risks of staying with the status quo are unacceptable while the risks of change are minimal. They will always go with the option that presents the lowest risk of failure because they fear failure more than they covet success. Minimize perceived risk, reassure, support and comfort steady prospects if you want them to change.

■ **C — Compliant**.

The compliant buyer adheres to all rules and regulations and focuses on product specifications, details and minutiae. If you turn on your personality with this buyer you will turn him off. With compliant buyers, slow down and get detail oriented. Don't push for the overall "Yes" until you have received a preliminary "Yes" at each previous step.

Let's dive into each personality type in more detail:

The Dominant Personality Type

Dominant persons, if they cannot find the door to a room, will barge through the wall to get inside. They are active people, fidgeting during presentations and preferring movement to being sedentary. Their leadership style is one of inspiration rather than perspiration. At the team meeting, they will announce the upcoming challenge and fire up the team with speechifying and cheerleading. If asked exactly how something is to be done, they may be stumped. Their strength is in "Can Do" rather than "How To."

My observation while delivering and explaining the DISC concept thousands of times matched what I had been told: Dominant persons represent 17 percent of the population of the United States of America.

They tend to be impatient. They are confident. If you praise them, they are not surprised that you think they are doing a good job because they are already sure that they are doing a good job. Your taking notice of that fact and remarking on it merely confirms what they already believed. As much as they expect praise, other personality types do not: "High I" persons are giddy with pleasure when receiving praise, "High S" persons are relieved to hear that they are doing a good job and "High C" persons know that they could have done the job better and believe that, next time, they will do it better. This indicates that a wise seller will make their High D presentation short and to the point and will be certain that they tread carefully when they suggest that this new product or service is an improvement on what the "High D" is already buying.

Dominant buyers are bold. They love to try new things. They wonder how they are going to change things and are strong believers in the adage that "insanity is doing the same thing over and over again and expecting different results." They will probably not know or care that this quote is attributed to Albert Einstein, preferring to believe that it originated with themselves.

Rather than resist change, they love to incite it. When Frank Sinatra sang, "I Did It My Way," the dominant personality type was surprised that he would consider doing it any other way. A wise seller positions a new idea so that the High D customer believes that he, the customer, thought it up.

High D people are good problem solvers, decision makers, goal achievers and leaders. A wise seller never says or does anything to try to outshine the High D buyer in any of these areas. When the spotlight comes on, as long as the news is good, let it shine on them alone. When the news is bad, hog the limelight and be prepared for the worst.

Pushing a High D customer is usually unnecessary as they lack caution. They boldly go where no one has gone before (pardon the split infinitive, but if the phrase is good enough for the opening for Star Trek, then it is good enough for this book). So, early direct closes work well. But, the wise seller guards against selling the High D an ineffective solution, taking advantage of the fact that these folks don't bother to check all the facts before beginning. If the solution fails to work, all blame will be attributed to the seller. High D buyers tend to overrun their own teammates, so closing the High D is, often times, the same as closing everyone on the team. The High D will steamroll over those who attempt to block this newly sold solution.

One cautionary note is this: High D buyers fear being taken advantage of. Since you are a seller — a person trying to "sell them something," you are going to be quickly assumed to be someone who is out to take advantage of them either with regard to price, terms and conditions or product quality. Guarantees work well then this occurs. But remember, they never want to allow anyone to take advantage of them. You are a seller. You are perceived by them as the number one person in their life to watch out for; your job, they may believe, is to take advantage of them. They fear you will overcharge them, deliver less than you promise, treat their competition with greater care or a myriad of other things where they come out on the short end of the stick. Your job is to make sure they are dissuaded of this belief and that their fear is calmed.

High D buyers thrive on status, power, prestige, authority and directness. Adopt this conduct of directness when selling to them. Build them up. Flatter them. Show deference to their wisdom, even if it is only a perceived wisdom. Never beat around the bush. Tell them the end of the story first. Don't give them many details unless they request them. Get to the point.

These are strong people. But, a strength, when over-extended, quickly becomes a weakness. Understand that your High D customers lack caution. They seldom check all the facts or details of a deal but will blame you when they are caught unawares by one of those details. They overrun people — a fact that surprises only them.

STUN High D people by tenaciously reverting to their primary unmet need. Sublimate your product or service when talking to the results your product or service will provide that clearly meet their unmet need. They like this approach. Unless they also possess a lot of High C tendencies — more on that later — avoid too much attention to detail in favor of a big picture view. Be absolutely direct and use direct closes. When direct closes fail, use choice closes. They are great at making quick decisions and love to choose between options. If there is only one option that will work for them, be careful when using a choice close approach because there will be disaster to deal with if they choose the option you had hoped they would avoid.

Use the QuickSell with High D's. It is made for their point of view as a buyer. It is critical that you never burn a bridge when dealing with a High D. It is acceptable to leave a bridge smoldering, however.

[79

Your directness may result in the occasional rebuke. That's OK. All you have to do is apologize for overstepping your bounds followed by an explanation that it is your passion for providing the solution to their unmet need that drove you to take a step too far.

Don't be arrogant. Leave that to them. They're top dog, highest on the totem pole. You can only be second. Show respect. Take notes when they pontificate. Be silent when they go on a tirade. Practice the objection handling skills that are outlined in Tool #8. Sell, don't tell. Don't be wishy-washy. Instead, be decisive.

When they rant and rave, keep your volume low. Speak softly and watch them tone themselves down. They love and thrive on conflict so you will need to either love it or, at the very least, tolerate it. Also, remember that whatever happens right now is in the past very soon. Unless they lose respect for you, a little bit of conflict is no problem.

You'll be fine unless you ever do something that causes this High D person to lose respect for you. When that happens, the relationship is irrevocably broken and the account may as well be reassigned. If the High D buyer doesn't respect you as a seller then you are finished. It's time to move on.

The Influencer Personality Type

Influencers or High I people love, well, people. They value personal relationships and friendship over all other things. Even standards take a back seat to relationships. Everybody loves High I people — except for High C people who, because of their focus on standards, believe that High I's are shallow and fluff. The problem with selling to High I people is that while they love you they also love your competitor. They like to buy from people they like and, since they like everyone, they would love to buy from everyone. If you want a bigger share of their business, you're going to have to become the person they love most. And, more challenging, you have to find a non-offensive way for them to love your competitor less.

How do you recognize them? Look for a smiling face in front of a warm and loving personality. When you are on their turf, they adopt "host" behavior by offering you a seat and a cup of coffee. They set aside the first few minutes of your encounter for small talk designed to break the ice. You'll notice their workspace is decorated with personal things such as photographs of their family, memorabilia of achievements or experiences and tokens of affection received from others. While High D folks will decorate their workplace to intimidate, High I folks will decorate theirs to welcome.

[81

They, like High D people, make up about 17 percent of the population. They are optimistic and find the good in things. Their cup is half full. They don't like complainers; they prefer to be around upbeat people who can see the bright side of things. They are like a little kid trapped in a room full of manure in that they will grab a shovel and begin to dig believing that there must be a pony in there somewhere.

I's are optimistic, gregarious, articulate, impulsive and, oftentimes, emotional. They are good at motivating others to do their finest work. They are very good communicators who can often describe their needs better than any other prospect you will encounter. They are both cooperative and interesting in doing "what's right for everyone."

When they overextend these attributes, their weaknesses quickly rise to the surface. They can and do become "easy marks."

You will find that, sometime in the past, your competitor will have taken advantage of them and, even if they realize what happened, they still express affection for that person. They seldom speak bluntly. This can and does work to your disadvantage when they hesitate to clearly tell you what is wrong with your proposal. They would prefer to criticize nothing, not realizing that their criticism, when not taken personally by you, would result in an improved offering and, therefore, improved results.

They get into trouble with time. They miss deadlines and sometimes show up late for appointments. Think about it: They have to have a bit of personal time with everyone and those minutes begin to add up. It's best to get appointments with them early in the day because of that. Of course, you may find that you arrive at their office before they do because, as you know, it takes time to stop and buy donuts for everyone on the way in... which they will often joyfully do.

Influencers fear the loss of social approval. If buying from you means that they have to make someone else uncomfortable or unhappy they will stall and stall and stall and retreat into doing nothing instead of doing something. They have a really hard time saying, "No." They substitute "Let me think about it," instead. The problem is that they don't think about it and eventually their lack of a decision reverts to a default "No" that they didn't have the courage to tell you up front.

They thrive on recognition, appreciation, acceptance and the freedom to do things their own way and on their own schedule. They like variety. They'd be happy to have a cup of coffee with you or have lunch as long as their company policy doesn't get in the way.

These are the people you love who you will come to hate if you don't handle them wisely. So, how should you behave? Always smile. Always be friendly. Listen; then listen more. That means you must ask lots of open questions. Never interrupt their answer even if that answer veers off topic.

When you sense that they are worried about accepting your proposal because it will "hurt" your competitor's feelings, remind them that since your competitor is truly their friend, that person will never begrudge them for doing what is in their and their company's best interest. Never, never, never criticize your competitor; you will not be forgiven for that.

Understand that it is fear of disapproval from others that grips the High I. They hesitate to do the bold thing because they fear it may upset others. If you are selling a bold solution, you will be required to do a lot of reassuring of a particular ilk: You must reassure them that their decision will make others happy and not upset anyone. They value popularity among those other persons and you must always find a way to communicate that your solution will enhance and not detract from that status.

Establish that you are the champion of great service after the sale. You will always be there for them because you care about them as people. You must be perceived as trustworthy so you can never promise more than you are capable of delivering.

When it is time to close you should expect a stall. They are champions of the "think about it" stall as they ponder how their decision will affect and impact other people in their organization. So, with High I buyers, you must become expert at delicate use of the urgency close.

"If you delay making this decision, it will hurt Charlie in Receiving and it will cause stress for Marilyn in Quality Control. I know you don't want that to happen. Can we move forward today so that no one on your team is stressed by a delay?"

Sellers must be cautious when they say, "Trust me." Since High D buyers instinctively don't trust sellers because they fear being taken advantage of and they have had sellers take advantage of them all their lives, High S buyers don't trust sellers other than their incumbent supplier because they fear change and High C buyers don't trust sellers because they have been burnt in the past by sellers who promised a product feature or a quality of service that they failed to deliver, High I buyers are vulnerable to trusting sellers because they see the good in people and they have faith that everyone, even sellers, has a good side that will surface if they just give them the opportunity. So, say "Trust me," to the High I, but don't say it to everyone else.

Of course you must never fail to deliver because if you fail that means their trust in you was misplaced. They will be personally hurt by that and by the fact that your failure led to their failure in the eyes of their team or their customers. So, don't make promises you can't keep. When the promise that you felt confident about making fails to happen because someone else failed you, never blame anyone else. Instead, heap the blame on your own shoulders and talk about how you trusted someone else who let you down, but that it was your own fault. The High I buyer, having experienced that very thing themselves, will heap empathy on you which will save your relationship.

Be careful: Always remember that everything that ever goes wrong is your fault; not the fault of someone else. When you adopt that stance, the High I buyer instinctively knows that you will never blame them for a failure either.

Take them to lunch, bring them a latte, and (even better) find a gesture of good will that you can offer up to a member of their family.

A congratulatory note on the date of one child's graduation from high school or another child's selection to the little league all-star team will endear you to them forever. The offer to make a phone call or write a letter to assist their college aged student in winning an internship at the business of another of your clients will gain you great affection which will be returned in the future.

At another time in my life, I was acquainted with a well-known personality who, from time to time, would be a guest on a late night television talk show. This person gave a great deal of thought to what story they would tell the host so as to deliver a memorable appearance. The talent coordinator for the talk show would even call to find out what that story might be to make sure it would sounded like something the host would find intriguing. Use this as a lesson as you prepare for your sales call with High I buyers. What story are you going to bring to tell that they will find intriguing? If you always have a story, you will

[85

be welcomed back in just the same way as David Letterman always welcomed Bill Murray or Regis Philbin to sit in "The Late Show" guest chair over and over and over again. Those guys made him laugh and he loved them for it. By the way, I miss Letterman because he made me laugh, too.

Smile.

The Steady Personality Type

If there is one defining characteristic of the Steady or High S personality it is this: They fear change. On the flip side, if there is one defining characteristic of any seller, it is that their job is to promote change — change from the status quo to what the he/she is selling. Therein lies the challenge with selling to S types: They wish you weren't there because buying from you will upset their apple cart and force a change. They prefer to not let go of the status quo.

How do you spot these buyers? Across the entire population, they represent 50 percent of all Americans. They have worked for their current employer for a long time. "How long have you worked here," you ask. "22 years," they say proudly. "Wow. You must love it here. Did you ever think of leaving and going elsewhere?" "Once."

Once in 22 years? High D buyers think of leaving and going elsewhere once every 22 days. High D and High I buyers usually have an updated resume lying in wait on their computer desktop, but the High S has no resume prepared at all. Rather than leave their current employer they are prone to wait it out knowing that their current situation will probably improve when their nemesis leaves before they do.

High S folks stay calm in a crisis. As a pilot, when the engine catches on fire, they radio air traffic control for the nearest place to land while simultaneously pulling the lever for the fire suppressant system. A High I pilot may be looking for a parachute and the High D pilot is cursing the mechanic for failing to prevent the flameout. You would prefer, if you consider it for a moment, to be in a High S piloted aircraft in a crisis. Before takeoff, over and over again — countless times — they go through the checklist while the High D pilot has a tendency to say, "Checklist? Nah; I don't need that anymore."

High S people tend to be overly hospitable. They allow others to take advantage of them. The house guest that would have been thrown out long ago by the rest of us remains in residence at the home of a High S host. They can, however, become possessive. "Where's my stapler?" they ask. They know which one is theirs because they used the label maker to affix their name to it. Of course, all the staplers belong to the company but the High S doesn't see it that way. If you ever intend to borrow their stapler, be sure to ask first. And, expect them to reply, "OK, but be sure to return it." If you use the last staple, for goodness sake, refill it before you return it or your next request to borrow something from them will be refused. It's their stuff.

High S people fear for their own job security. If a boss threatens a High S by saying, "If you don't get this right, I'm going to fire you," that High S person will become petrified and, perhaps, paralyzed. If the boss similarly threatens a High D, the response is different: "Go ahead. It will be your loss."

In their office, you will find pictures of the family they personally brought in to display. Meanwhile, the High D has lost the pictures of their family while the High C is going to display their family photos once they locate the perfect frame. The High I's are lucky to get the photos into their office as they probably lost their camera and forgot to use their phone for that purpose — their family photo was a gift from those who appear in the picture.

High S buyers are consistent performers not prone to highs and lows such as you might find with High D buyers. They are team oriented and prefer to blend in rather than stand out, another major difference between them and D's or I's. Generally agreeable and amiable, they are nonetheless difficult to persuade if what you're selling represents a departure from what they are currently doing. They prefer a stable environment rather than one which embraces the unknown.

They are patient to a fault, tolerating what is rather than embracing what might be.

When the High D says, "Let's do something even if it's wrong," the High S (and to a similar degree the High C buyer) says, "Let's do nothing unless it's right." Rather than having a passion to win, they are sometimes held back by a fear of loss.

Like all customers, they are need-focused but they are cooperative to the point where the idea of a win/win relationship appeals to them. They will not begrudge the fact that you make a profit from their business as long as they make a profit as well. Not greedy, they tend to nibble less and are prepared to give and take, compromise and swap what's good for you for what's good for them. They don't want to take advantage of you as long as you don't take advantage of them.

These folks are steady and relaxed, calm in crisis, unhurried even under pressure and never eager to be the early adopter pioneer. New ideas should be first proven to work with others, thank you.

These are loyal people who give back because they appreciate what they have been given. Uniformity and consistency are important to them. Rocking the boat is not something they are comfortable doing. Risk taking is acceptable only once the risk has been thoroughly evaluated, weighed and deemed to be so low as to be non-existent. One problem in this regard is the fact that they are prone to trusting whom they shouldn't and are vulnerable to half-truths, exaggerations and even lies that they are told. Once they experience betrayal at the hands of an unethical seller, they never forget that each buy decision could come with disaster hidden from them by a dishonest seller.

[89

This causes them to miss opportunities to hit a home run because they don't want to ever be accused of having swung at a bad pitch. Steal a base? You've got to be kidding; the odds are that they will be thrown out. It's better to wait and run only when the next batter has stroked a clean single allowing a risk free advance.

They need to trust you. But how?

First, reassure them at every turn. Point out — and be ready to prove — how your offering has worked flawlessly for others in similar situations. Show how your firm has performed in the past when the chips were down. Offer testimonials, but be cautious that the source of your testimonials aren't flamboyant High D or High I endorsers. The best testimonial you can offer them is from a fellow High S or High C person who is calm in their praise and not prone to over exaggeration. Sell them on what you have done in the past and reassure them that nothing has changed that would keep you from performing at that or a higher level going forward.

To get off to a good start, when you first communicate with a High S buyer, find something that you can promise and then quickly deliver. For example, if they seem lukewarm to your initial contact, promise to send them a testimonial or proof source about a claim you made and then, quickly, deliver it. This shows that you promptly do what you say you are going to do and is the first step toward building trust.

Don't speak ill of their current supplier even if they give you that opening. Instead, just nod your head and speak humbly of what you can and will do for them. This is the customer who will most appreciate your empathy for their plight and problems. "I am so sorry that you have to deal with that," you might say. "One thing I will promise you and guarantee is that if you work with me, I will be there to see that doesn't happen to you again." If you can make their problems disappear, you will reappear on their preferred supplier list over and over again. The problem for you is this: Your sales cycle time with this buyer will be longer than you will like. You will have to be quietly and calmly persistent as you subtly push them to make changes.

High S buyers are the best stallers among all customers. Disliking change as they do, they constantly want to think about it and take your proposal to others for approval. Understand that once those others approve what you are proposing, the consequence of any ultimate failure of your offering no longer rests on the shoulders of this High S buyer but has instead been transferred to others. In that way the High S has alleviated themselves from the consequence of failure.

In Tool #10, "Defeating Stalls," we will discuss tactics for both the "Think About It Stall" and the "Committee Stall" (taking your proposal to many others for approvals). Read and reread that chapter when you are preparing to sell to the High S buyer. One enhancement that works well when fighting High S stalls is the "Extra Mile" approach. "I'm willing to go the extra mile for you. I will do this at no charge to prove to you that the level of our dedication to your business success is unmatched." Then, go the extra mile for them. You will be rewarded later. The problem is that later will come much later than you would like.

The Compliant Personality Type

If you've reviewed this chapter in sequence and you are waiting for this section on the Compliant Personality Type or High C's — and you are a High C yourself — you know that I am going to tell you that High C personalities represent 16 percent of the population. You noted it when I said that High D's and High I's each comprised 17 percent and that

High S folks represented half the population so your mind automatically performed the calculation and you know that 16 percent is what remains. However I am now going to frustrate you by saying that High C's are also 17 percent of us. How can that be?

It can be because I rounded. The actual statistics are 16 2/3, 16 2/3, 50 and 16 2/3 percent, respectively, which, as you can quickly compute, equals the 100 percent that must be the ultimate total.

High D people who are reading this book are asking themselves what I am talking about here and who cares anyway. High I people and High S people get it and accept my rounding as a step which simplifies the point. But, High C people are bothered by the inaccuracy and inattention to detail only brought to light at this late time.

Here's my point: High C people are accurate to a fault. They are tactful, however, when pointing out my obvious inattention to detail. Details are their strong suit. They have the operations manual close at hand at all times. High D's ask, "What manual?" High I's lost theirs. High S people are slowly but surely revising the manual to more accurately reflect what is currently happening. But High C people look upon the manual as the Holy Grail that, if all embraced, would ensure quality across the enterprise.

High C people have an uncanny gut feeling about whether or not something is going to work. If they say, "I don't think that is going to work," you should listen to their explanation as to why and not react negatively because they failed to simply accept the new idea. They are analytical people and they have made it a habit to think through the impending change with a step by step approach that leaves nothing uninspected.

They can, and often do, become overly precise. This tendency causes them to procrastinate and miss fleeting opportunities because their tendency to analyze before acting takes too much time.

They don't delegate well. Their motto? "If you want it done right, do it yourself." They fear criticism of their work, however. So, they will check and re-check until they are confident of their own perfection. They have the highest standards and will demand perfection from you almost as much as they demand it of themselves.

Prove it. They are rigid when it comes to change and they will demand data, not anecdotes. They are process oriented and you will follow their process or you will fail. When others say, "close enough," they will shake their head in disbelief.

They are self-centered and they don't care whether or not they reach a win/win result with you. They would prefer a win for themselves and a tiny loss for you. That's better than our High D buyers, however, in that the High D wants a giant win for themselves and a complete defeat for you.

C's are very need focused and require vast amounts of detail. You will find that the route to building a relationship with this buyer is paved with data, detail and facts. They will ask for proof, information from an unbiased source, and the opportunity to test or pilot your offering. Going in with small talk about the weather or last week's opening blockbuster at the multiplex is the wrong way to go. Get down to business. Stow your smile; it won't help you in this office and, in fact, might even hurt as the High C may label you as being overly emotional if you emote.

[93

For them, the definition of the word "Quality" is "adherence to standards." They have the highest of standards. So, when you want to impress them, do it by showing a clear understanding and mastery of their corporate standards and that you've done your homework to prove that your product or service measures up in every way. Quality is what you're selling if you want to be successful with a High C buyer.

They are slow to change, they fear mistakes or errors and they will have calculated the downside

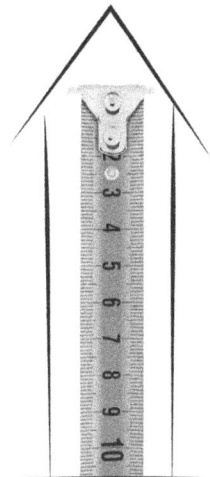

of your relationship with more focus than on the potential upside. As you talk about all the benefits of your proposal, they will be seeing all the true negatives in it. In our upcoming chapter on overcoming objections, pay close attention to the strategies on true negative objections and master them. Acknowledge the downside and be prepared to show the odds of success substantially or overwhelmingly outweigh the odds of failure. Then, expect them to want you to provide contingency planning for failure even though those plans will probably never be needed.

If you want to be mentally ahead of them, you should consider reversing your presentation to highlight everything that could go wrong and how you can avoid that rather than the more typical approach of highlighting everything that will go right.

Before you can close, you will want to reassure them that buying from you is the best approach to risk management and risk avoidance. If you ever see that they have made a mistake or error, please don't point it out unless you find a way to blame that miscalculation on yourself. High C buyers don't like to lose face and being caught in an error is the most unforgivable mistake they can make. If they, at your hands, lose face then you, at your hands, lose the account.

Have a binder full of proof and have it with you at all times.

You can't afford to have them demand proof and say that you'll go find it. Have it now or risk being tossed onto a pile to which they never have time to return. Their "To-Do" list is a long one; their roster of unread emails is lengthy and their pile of documents to be read is high. If you miss the moment, you may not ever get it again.

At closing time, you'll need to push. Just be sure you push with facts and that you can justifiably point out that the downside of inaction is much greater than the downside of saying "Yes." They need reassurance that they are doing the right thing. Give it to them and be prepared to back up your claims and key points. Never say, "Trust me," because they won't and, frankly, don't.

Do not overpromise. Instead, under-promise and over-deliver.

If you're a rookie or not well versed in technical details, bring your product experts, engineers and technicians along. Do not attempt to gain a personal relationship. Keep it strictly business. Leave your attempts at humor at the door.

[95

They will buy from you when they are ready, but they won't be ready until they have analyzed, re-analyzed and then verified. This is a multiple call type of buyer. Take it one step at a time. They won't buy low quality at a low price preferring to buy what their standards dictate at a favorable price.

Follow up. Business reviews are of great value. Reports, trend-spotting, early warning of potential problems and attention to minutiae will raise you to the top of their preferred supplier list.

Indeed, knowing the intricacies of each personality type may seem daunting, but it is critical if you wish to sell your solution to a variety of buyers. Once you internalize these characteristics, recognizing and distinguishing the High D from the High I, High S or High C will become second nature and will lead to improved results for you.

WHAT I WOULD HAVE DONE DIFFERENTLY
IF I KNEW THEN WHAT I KNOW NOW

Now that I know and recognize the various personality types, there are changes to my sales approach that I would have made. Namely, I would have spent more time looking at my prospects' personality types. That is not to say that I would have given any less attention to identification of their unmet needs. Instead, it means that I would couple my maniacal focus on their unmet need with a nod to their desired approach. I would have become a mirror of sorts with them; so, if they acted as a High D when dealing with me then I would have acted as a High D in return — just making sure that my High D approach was coupled with clear deference to their superior position to me.

Similarly, if my client was a High I, I would have been much more patient at "small talk" time when calling on them. As a High D, High I blend person myself, I enjoyed a little bit of relationship building, but was always eager to get to the point and make the sale. I needed to slow down and take in the time with this type of buyer, listening to their stories even though my mind was saying, "Hurry up, hurry up; finish your story

THEN... CONTINUED

so I can sell you something." Also, with the High I customer, I would have been much more tolerant of his loyalty to my competitor and never ever have fallen into the trap of criticizing my competition's offerings, service or ethics. I might have laid the groundwork for my customer to criticize my competition but I would never have done it myself.

Then, with the High S customer, I would have been more patient and more willing to settle for a smaller slice of the business to get started. I would have attempted to resist closing on the entire proposal in favor of getting agreement on a portion of it instead. I would have respected this person's fear of failure rather than becoming frustrated at their lack of enthusiasm for a big success.

Finally, with the High C customer, I would have completely altered my personality to become low key and detail oriented. I would have come armed with documents in a heavy case rather than with a brief presentation deck. And, I would have left humor, sarcasm and even a hint of irreverence out in my car in the parking lot.

WHAT YOU SHOULD DO RIGHT NOW

Look closely at your toughest customer and determine what his/her primary personality tendency is: D, I, S or C.

- If they are a High D, adopt the suggestions listed in this Tool and see if you don't get better results more quickly.

- If you identify High I customers, turn on your own High I side when you call on them — if you don't instinctively have a High I side to your personality, you must consciously create and then wear a High I mask when you call on them. You are capable of doing that because you realize that you only need to wear that mask for a short time — the time you are in their physical presence. You can do it if you understand that you must only do it for a few minutes.

- If your client matches the descriptions of High S buyers, prepare to slow down and go step by step on your quest for success. To do that, you will have to figure out how to take the big decision you require from them and break it down into a series

NOW... CONTINUED

of smaller decisions, each one easier to make because it carries with it less risk. And, for each small decision, be prepared to provide testimonials from similarly cautious sources, proof of your claims and reassurance of your presence at every step of the changes you require for this person to change from what they are doing to what you want them to do.

- And, if you identify High C prospects, prepare to amaze them with your mastery of detail. Have the patience for a long haul toward the ultimate close, knowing that your victory will come in small steps and never in giant leaps.

Don't forget, when it comes to closing the sale, set aside your own personality tendencies and, instead, sell to the primary personality type of your customer.

You can't change them, so you must change yourself instead. If you would like more on DISC, take a look at the ej4 video series on the topic located at STUNselling.com/personality_types.

100]

TOOL #6

Selling to Different Customer Roles

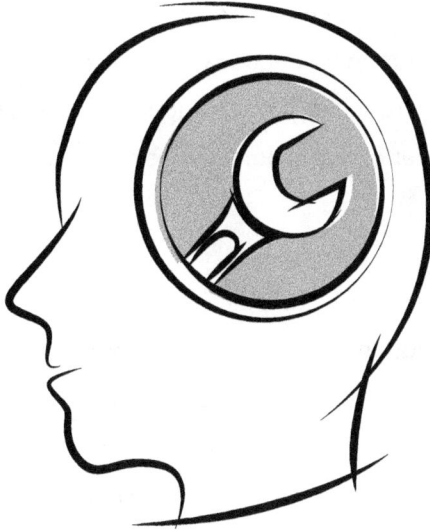

Here's What You're Going to Learn

In a complex sale or among the cast members of sale a to a Committee, different people represent different outlooks on your product or service. One person may be the actual user of your product. Another may determine how your product interacts with other products that the buyer's company already uses. Another may be simply the money person deciding if the price is competitive. Another may have a close relationship with your company while still another may have a close relationship with your competition. These people all look at what you are selling from a different perspective. Most importantly, they each have a different unmet need.

You must address all roles and STUN each one in a different manner if you hope to close the sale.

THE POINT

One set of features and benefits doesn't fit all different buyers inside a single prospect company because they each have different unmet needs. You need to customize your selling story for each person's needs. For each one, without a need, don't proceed.

Customers and prospects have different people playing different roles inside their organizations. Each of these people have different unmet needs. They have different perspectives on their business. They are held accountable and are responsible for different objectives.

There are people who think only about economics or profitability. There are others who think only about sales or marketing of their product or service offerings and are primarily concerned with quantity rather than margin. Others think only about how they produce their product or deliver their service. They don't consider economics or quantity but, instead, think about whether or not they can even produce the product to an acceptable standard.

Economic buyers, then, have a different need than marketing buyers or production buyers. But each one plays a role in whether or not you are successful in your sales effort to their organization.

If you get into a feature/benefit discussion with an economic buyer, it had better be economic features and benefits that you discuss. They do not care about the nuance of production. They are looking at costs. Similarly, a feature/benefit discussion with a production buyer about how well their output will sell to their ultimate customer is a waste of your breath. They don't do that and, if the product doesn't sell, well, that's not their problem.

But, it gets even more complicated when you figure out that each of these buyers — economic, marketing, production, etc., have multiple needs. The economic buyer cares about costs, sure, but also about margins. The marketing buyer cares about feature/benefit points of difference that he can deliver to his market — and those are going to be derived in part from your feature/benefit points of difference. He's into bells and whistles rather than sticker shock. You have multiple features and benefits to discuss and he cares only about the ones that ultimately make a difference to his customer. The production buyer looks at your feature/benefit points of difference in a different way: She wants to see how they enhance or detract from her manufacturing needs. And, she has a lot of those.

These multiple needs are not all equal. Some are more urgent than others. Knowing which is most urgent means that you must not only know all the needs one of these buyers has, you must also arrange them into a hierarchy.

I am reminded of Abraham Maslow's Heirarchy of Needs, a psychological theory first discussed in the 1943 publication of an article in *Psychological Review* entitled "A Theory of Human Motivation." Maslow greatly expanded his theory two years later in a book entitled *Motivation and Personality*.

As sellers, what could be more important for you and me than understanding our prospects' motivation and personality? Motivation is simple. Look at the word and break it into two parts and you'll see what I mean. "Motiv" is the first half. A motive is a reason. "Ation" is the second half. Add the letter "C" to that and you get the word "Action." So, I'd say that motivation is nothing more than a *reason for action*. According to

$$\text{motiv} \ \overset{c}{\underset{\wedge}{\text{ation}}}$$

Maslow, needs must be met and the most urgent needs must be met first —before other needs even matter.

Simply put, we must uncover every need a particular buyer has and arrange those needs into a hierarchy so we can address the most urgent one first. Our customer will not hear what we say if we are addressing his second most urgent need while his brain is focused on his first most urgent need. We've got to talk about what he is concerned about. Never say, "I'll get to that in just a minute after I finish explaining this." He won't hear what you say about *this* when his brain is thinking about *that*. You must STUN in the proper sequence.

As for personality, we just learned in Tool #5 about four different personality types. Suffice it to say that we must not only address the most urgent need first, but we must also address it taking into account how our prospect thinks about that urgent need based on his/her personality type. Remember D, I, S, C.

We have to understand how many decision makers are involved in our sale, as well as what needs each of those decision makers has and then arrange each of those needs into a list with the most important unmet need at the top of each person's list.

We address the most important unmet need first and only with the buyer who possesses and cares about that need.

Once that need is deemed met, it makes no sense to discuss it any further. We attempt to close.

Maslow said that humans care most about basic physiological needs. Take air to breathe as an example. That is the most urgent need of all humans. We care about air to breathe more than we care about anything else. Unless, of course, we have ample air to breathe. Then we don't care about it at all. We consider it a met need and, therefore, it is no longer at the forefront of our minds. As such, we move to our next most urgent need. Maslow might say that is security. Once that need is met, the next most urgent unmet need moves to the forefront. To motivate, to give our prospect a reason for action, is to address and meet the most urgent unmet need in that prospect's mind when it is most urgent. Once it is moved to the met column, move on.

Move on to what? Move on to the close. When a need is met in the mind of a prospective buyer, that buyer sends you a signal. That signal may be a nod of the head, a verbal cue such as, "I see what you mean," or an unfolding of folded arms. What do you do when you get that signal — which we call a buying sign? You close. Of course, there are other unmet needs in this prospect's head but who cares? If they aren't important — because they are far down his hierarchy — you may

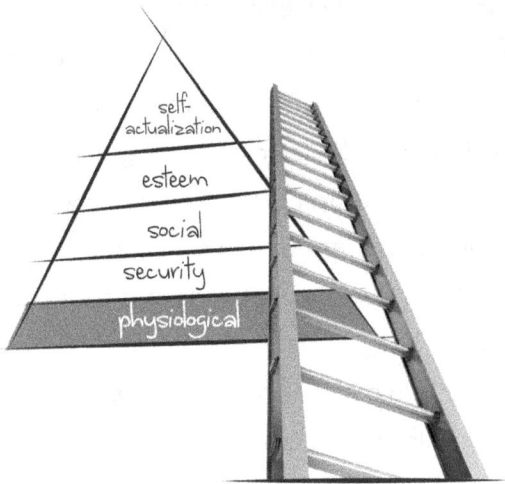

be wasting your time covering off on them. The buyer will let you know by giving you an objection if you attempt to close prematurely. That's not a problem. Read Tool #8 on objections for more on this point.

The key takeaway from Maslow is this: Don't talk to a buyer about a less urgent need first. Go to the most urgent need first.

Of course, before you call on any one of these buyers, you need to gather information. What are the unmet needs of each key player in the prospect's organization? Without a need, don't proceed.

But how do you do this?

If you will be presenting to a committee, do your homework. First, talk to your primary contact and find out the names and roles of each person who will be in your audience. It is reasonably safe to assume that once you find that "Lonnie" is the CFO that "Lonnie" will respond to economic benefits and not to operational ones. Similarly, when you learn that "Mitch" is the marketing guru, he will respond to traffic and transaction metric benefits. "Jacqueline" who is the merchandise buyer will be wowed by design but not necessarily by payment terms.

There is more. Can you not call your contact at this organization or some other vendor with whom you have a relationship and say, "Tell me about Mitch." Let that person coach you about how to approach him. What you want to know is whether or not Mitch is a High D or a High C personality type. If you can learn that, you can deliver your traffic metric benefit in either a bold narrative or a highly detailed explanation and know that you will have a better chance of gaining his endorsement. If you know that Lonnie is a High S, you can frame your economic points in a way that promises low risk of down side exposure rather than you would if he was a High D when high odds of a financial windfall would be more persuasive.

The key here is to combine role and personality type and literally make eye contact with that decision maker when you are delivering a custom benefit in a personality-appropriate manner. A question following each benefit statement, such as, "That would be critical for you to endorse this proposal, would it not?" will solicit agreement accompanied by a clearly perceived nod of the head. We will talk in more detail in the next chapter on closing about these "nod questions" and the concept of "nod momentum."

It is important to note that the bigger the company is, the more likely people in economic roles are to care little or nothing about the people in operational roles and vice versa. If you are selling to a small or medium sized organization, it is more likely that role players in one silo at least have some affinity for other role players in other silos. If a corporate culture is that people are encouraged to have had cross-functional backgrounds, that company is likely to have silos that are more porous or conjoined one with another.

Should you ever find yourself in room full of MBA types who represent the venture capital owner of your target, they may care nothing at all about long-term operational benefits and, instead, be focused only upon short-term financial metrics that will yield for them a higher stock price when the entity soon goes public.

The point here is simple and profound: If a benefit doesn't STUN —satisfy their unmet need—then don't bring it up. But, in a group setting, you must bring it up because you have a diverse audience. You speak directly to and in the appropriate way to the person who will be STUNned and then move on. You'll only close a sale when each psychological circle is closed. Unmet needs followed by features enhanced by benefits that meet those needs; that's the formula for every buyer no matter what their role or personality.

[107

For example, do you know how each person views their current business situation? Are they of the opinion that "their numbers" are solid? Then you needn't address that point. Are they worried that some competitor of theirs is a threat to "their numbers?" If that is the case, your feature/benefit discussion about how they can beat their completion just vaulted to the top of their hierarchy.

When you strategize a presentation, you must match your solution with each buyer's situation. And, you must sequence what you will present in the same order that those situational unmet needs occur in your buyer's brain.

That means that while the features of your solution may be the same, you must remember that you are pairing those features up with different needs held by different people. And, most important of all, you must translate each of the benefits derived from those features into benefits that match up with that person's unmet needs. The same feature may—and probably does—deliver different benefits to different buyers. You're the translator.

You say to the economic buyer: "You need this and I have this thing to offer. It delivers this benefit." To the production buyer you say, "You need this other thing. I have this same thing to offer. For you, it delivers this other benefit."

I lived this truth thousands of times with people who sold to Walmart.

Walmart has different buyers. Some are in Bentonville, Arkansas, at corporate headquarters. Others are in each local store. Some stores are in rich markets while others are in less affluent locations. Walmart store managers are more concerned with metrics (overall store volume and margin) than are Walmart department managers who care more about out of stocks and labor expense.

When we would try to sell in a pallet display of, for example, Pepsi products, we would have to take into consideration who we were talking to. An economic buyer in Bentonville wanted a cost advantage, but didn't care much about keeping shelves or displays full. A store manager cared about product selection and how that would impact her store's sales volume. A department manager cared about how much service frequency we had in mind for him so that he never had to lift a finger to keep the shelf or display or pallet full. The check-in person at the back door cared about whether or not the product count matched the order documents and how swiftly and cleanly we got the pallets off our truck and neatly through her back room and out to the selling floor.

Never make the mistake of overlooking the importance of this check-in person even though they are lower on the customer organization chart and seemingly without power. They have a powerful "veto" vote with the person or persons who do have power. Keeping them STUNned will prevent them from rocking the boat with a buyer who is higher up the decision-making ladder and increase the odds that you will be successful.

Talking to a back room person about case cost was never considered because she didn't care. Talking to the Bentonville buyer about what we did with the shrink wrap after we unloaded our delivery vehicle was met with deaf ears. Each buyer has a different urgent unmet need and, in a complex sale where there are multiple people to keep happy, we forget that at our ultimate peril.

[109

I remember presenting Pepsi, Anheuser-Busch, Dolly Madison and Sara Lee products to different buyers at the headquarters level of the Walmart corporation. We talked about product costs. When we got to Target, we talked about store traffic. Walmart had all the traffic it could handle so that very urgent need was met. Target needed traffic above all else because without store traffic, Target was out of business.

Target would lose money on a product if it would bring a customer into their store that might otherwise shop at Walmart. Walmart, confident that it had the loyalty of its customers, cared instead about how much profit would be made from each unit they sold. This changed over time. The key to selling was to know what buyer you were talking to (economic, marketing, production, whatever) and what unmet need was paramount in their mind.

WHAT I WOULD HAVE DONE DIFFERENTLY
IF I KNEW THEN WHAT I KNOW NOW

I would have taken each "canned" sales pitch I was taught and customized it to the role played by the person to whom I was pitching. No two presentations inside a customer organization would have been alike.

WHAT YOU SHOULD DO RIGHT NOW

Make a list of all the buyers in a particular target enterprise delineating who are they and what role they play. Then, make a list of all the unmet needs each one has. Then, arrange those needs into a hierarchy for each person.

[111]

You'll have to meet the most urgent needs of each one if you want to succeed. That means, you'll have to learn how to translate the benefits of every feature you have so that they satisfy the unmet need of the person to whom you're currently talking. And, don't forget to discuss those unmet needs in the order in which they are lined up in the prospect's brain.

For more on this topic, take a look at this short ej4 video, "Selling to Different Customer Roles," located at STUNselling.com/customer_roles.

112]

TOOL #7

Closing the Sale

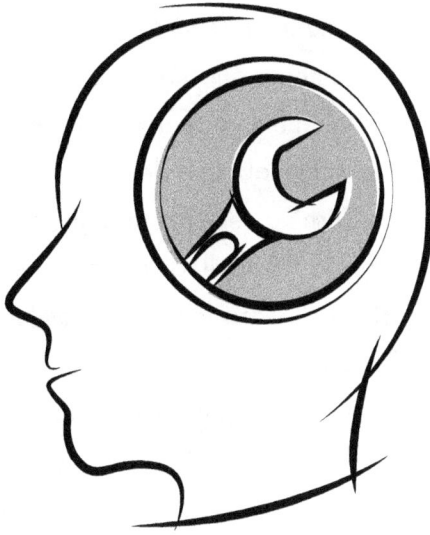

Here's What You're Going to Learn

It's not a sale until it's closed.

And, while it is true that there are three (or, perhaps, three hundred) different ways to close a sale, it is the "set up" for the close that truly makes the difference.

THE POINT

To increase your success rate, first set it up, then close. Nod momentum is the key.

While I was at Josten's/American Yearbook Company in 1973, I was expertly tutored by Dave Ramberg and Wendell "The Silver Fox" Dayton. These guys were in their late fifties or early sixties back then and knew everything there was to know about sales and, in particular, selling high school yearbook publishing services to high school principals and yearbook advisors. Dave and Wendell ran a semi-annual event known as "New Man's School" at the Howard Johnson's Hotel in Topeka, Kansas, where AYC was then headquartered.

I had initially joined AYC right after being fired from KOAM-TV in Pittsburg, Kansas, as the Director of Audio Visual Services. I vividly remember that the offer from Paul Erickson was for an annual salary of $10,800 and I held out for $11,200 and got it. At one "New Man's School," Dave had a touch of laryngitis, Wendell was occupied somewhere else and I got pressed into service to act as the voice of the training. Dave would, in a whisper, tell me what to say to the assembled "New Men" and I would loudly do so.

[As an aside, if you are wondering whether or not I was going to address the title, "New Man's School," rest assured that I am. In those days, there were no female sales representatives at AYC. Our sales"men" were primarily former teachers, coaches and principals who wanted to do something different and more lucrative from their careers in education. That was the profile then. Gender discrimination was the norm and, for that, I apologize here formally and vocally.]

New Man's School was an intense week-long sales and product training event with long days filled to overflowing with information that culminated on Fridays in a video-taped, peer-judged, mock sales presentation.

My major in college was marketing and the idea of selling things was intriguing to me as long as I didn't have to do the selling. More accurately, it was intriguing as long as I didn't have to close. I could do product development to satisfy customer needs and I was always good at describing features and converting those into benefits. Objection theory was a strength but tactical execution of that theory was more problematic because I didn't much care for conflict.

Closing was out of the question. Closing petrified me. Closing meant laying it all on the line, all at once, risking everything, asking a pointed question and inviting rejection in the form of one of those aforementioned objections. Sales was not for me. The reason was simple: I was petrified at the idea of asking for the order.

But money called. At AYC in those days, there were two legendary salesmen: Frank Wright operated from Wichita, Kansas, and Jimmy Combs was based in St. Louis, Missouri. Legend had it (and no one in a position to do so disputed it) that these two each earned over $100,000 per year in commissions. That amount was $88,800 more than I earned and, frankly, more money than I had ever dreamed of.

[115

I determined that I would someday become a Frank Wright or a Jimmy Combs. Even with my fear of closing, I vowed to someday, in some way, make it happen.

Dave and Wendell asked me if I would consider a new job at AYC and become the first "National Sales Recruiter." My job would be to find qualified candidates to fill open sales representative jobs and present a slate to the regional sales managers for final selection. I jumped at the chance. Two remarkable things happened to me in that job. The first one was that I included a qualified female candidate for a sales position and the second was that I submitted myself as a candidate when the right open territory came up. She got hired and so did I.

That meant that I had to attend one final New Man's School (sadly, not renamed because of her inclusion). I aced that week except for one thing. I could present and present in the most eloquent of manners, but I
could not close. Dave saw my nervous demeanor and, in an unforgettable move, gave me a nickname, "Sweaty Hand Red." By way of explanation, as mentioned in an earlier part of this book, my hair was red and my palms would perspire so much from nerves that I would rub them on my trouser leg to dry them before reaching out to shake hands with my fellow "New Man" who was playing the part of my prospect during the role plays.

I tell you this extremely long story (which has been great fun for me to recall) for one reason and one reason only: Know that great closers are not born — they are made. Today, I am a great closer. I am great because I learned the process, the psychology, the timing and the strategies to implement for success. I'm really good at closing today and, if you're not, you can be tomorrow if you'll follow along with me in this most important of chapters: Closing.

First, like a strikeout pitch, a close must first be set up to be effective. I once heard an interview with Nolan Ryan, all time major league strikeout leader. As I recall it, a breathless interviewer with a microphone to his mouth asked, "What is it about the pitch you throw for the third strike that makes you the greatest strikeout pitcher of all time?" Again, as I recall it, a somewhat bemused Ryan responded by saying, "It's not the third strike I throw that makes me the greatest strikeout pitcher. It's the pitch I throw before that."

I will never forget how profoundly I was struck by that. He was saying that his success was due in large measure to setting up that final step. If he could throw heat where the batter was not expecting heat to come, he would be off balance and swing and miss.

In closing a sale, a similar thing happens. I believe that it's not the close that counts. I believe it's the set-up for the close. Certainly, the close itself must be great, but it's getting the prospect set up to say "Yes" that's critical.

[117

Nod Momentum

You may be wondering, how does the set-up work? It works through use of my favorite tactic in sales: Creation of "Nod Momentum." My theory is this: It is quite difficult to say "No" when your head is nodding up and down. My tactical joy comes from getting people to nod. Nodding leads to "Yes."

You want to become a great seller who makes lots of money. Am I right?

Is there any chance you just thought — and maybe even said out loud — "Yes" accompanied by a nod of your head? If you did, you just discovered my tactic. To get someone to nod their head up and down, simply make an unmet need statement ("You want to become a great seller who makes lots of money.") and follow that with a nod question ("Am I right?")

Then, wait for it. The nod will come. It is creepy how well this works.

> *To the grocery store decision maker:* "You'd like to draw new customers to your store, wouldn't you?" Nod.

> *To the restaurant manager:* "You'd like to drive up average check size during happy hour, wouldn't you?" Nod.

> *To the training manager:* "You want to get your accident rate to fall. True?" Nod.

> *To the general counsel:* "You'd like to eliminate discrimination claims arising from ill-advised interview questions, wouldn't you?" Nod.

> *To the purchasing agent:* "Saving money on fuel appeals to you, doesn't it?" Nod.

I could go on and on. If you verbally present an unmet need to a customer — an unmet need that you have researched and know to exist — and follow that with a nod question, you will get that nod. I promise. That's one nod.

Then, without hesitation, you succinctly deliver a fact about the product or service you are selling — called a "feature," and then without hesitation expand on that by pointing out the benefits that feature delivers to the buyer and then, again without hesitation, ask another nod question, you're going to get nod number two.

> *To the grocery store decision maker:* "You'd like to draw new customers to your store, wouldn't you?" Nod. "By advertising these 12-packs at this price (feature) you'll get customers to abandon your competition and come here for that bargain (benefit). That's what you want, isn't it?" Ah, there it is, nod number two.

> *To the restaurant manager:* "You'd like to drive up average check size during happy hour, wouldn't you?" Nod. "By running our 'Bucket 'o Buds' promotion, a pair of beer drinkers will buy five instead of four which will drive up their check size. That's what you're after, right?" Nod number two.

> *To the training manager:* "You want to get your accident rate to fall. True?" Nod. "By implementing our online 'Back Smarts' program, your people will end up with fewer strains and less time off or light duty time so your costs go down while your productivity goes up. That's critical for you, isn't it?" Nod number two.

[119

> *To the general counsel:* "You'd like to eliminate discrimination claims arising from ill-advised interview questions, wouldn't you?" Nod. "By running our 'Interviewing Skills' training, your interviewers will learn the correct and better way to get what they need from applicants without asking discriminatory or litigious questions. Fewer complaints means legal cost savings for you, right?" Nod number two.

> *To the purchasing agent:* "Saving money on fuel appeals to you, doesn't it?" Nod. "Using our 'Driver Skills' training cuts down on things like jackrabbit starts and excessive idling which means less fuel for you to buy. You save money. That's critical these days, wouldn't you say?" Nod number two.

Think about what is happening here. First, I am making an unmet need statement and then confirming that I am correct in what I said by following with a confirming question — a nod question. Since I am right because I have done my homework, I get a "Yes" in one form or another accompanied by a slight or vigorous nod of the head. That's nod number one. Second, I am making a feature statement — concisely and without much detail — accompanied by a slightly longer and more explanatory benefit statement. Since the benefit statement I make is a perfect satisfier for the unmet need I set it up with, that second nod question is a, well, snap. I get a second nod.

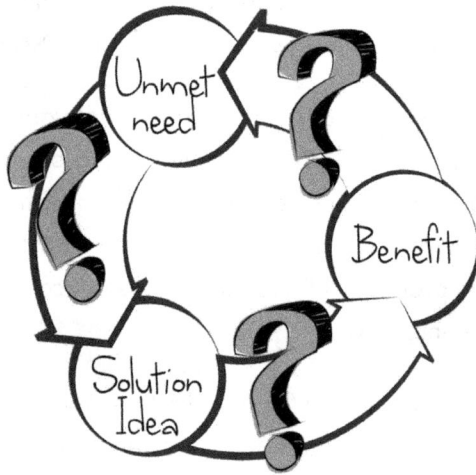

I have now, in very few seconds, created an unassailably accurate set-up of what I am selling and why my prospect needs it. I have received — because it is logical and I deserve to receive them — two nods. These two nods set up my strikeout pitch: "Can we ink a deal?"

For this prospect to stop nodding up and down and start shaking back and forth requires a complete change of pace for his neck, his head and his brain. Countless times, I have seen customers just keep on nodding. In some situations, the deal is done there.

In others, the prospect nods but uses the dreaded word: "But." The definition of "but" is: What I just said doesn't count. Let me show you:

"You look good in that tie, but..."
You don't look good in that tie.

"Your service was excellent, but..."
Your service had a fatal flaw.

"My flight was on time, but..."
Somehow, I wasn't.

But, if your second nod is followed by a "but," all is not lost. On the contrary, now the real selling begins. Real selling does not begin until you hear, "No." Using this set-up of nod momentum — which all follows the precise pattern we introduced to you early in the form of the QuickSell — gets you a deal or an objection which will ultimately lead you back to this same psychological circle for another go round.

[121]

Whatever objection you hear is greeted with an unmet need statement.

The prospect says, "Your price is outrageous." This is either a misunderstanding objection (if it's not true) or a true negative objection (if it is true).

You say, "You're looking for better value, is that it?" Nod.

You continue, "You won't save on the beer but you'll make extra profit on the extra bottle meaning the money comes to you from revenue rather than expense savings. It's the extra profit that you're after — no matter from where it comes. Right?" Second nod. Now close: "Can I order the buckets so we can get started?" Wait for it: Here comes the third nod — the trifecta! You're the winning jockey.

The prospect says, "I don't know; I've got table tents for appetizers to try to increase the check average." That's an indifference objection.

You say, "You'll take an increased check size from either appetizers or beer or both, won't you?" There's your third nod. Bam!

Close again. "How many buckets do you need; is 50 enough?" Wait for it: Here comes the fourth nod—you've got a deal.

You can do this process after every objection you hear to set up a close. If you start with the QuickSell pattern and use nod momentum to set up a close, you have created a rhythm of selling. You have created nod momentum. When you attempt to close, you get one of two things. You get a "Yes." Or, you get a "No," accompanied by an objection. You tackle that objection correctly and you'll find that the end of the answer to

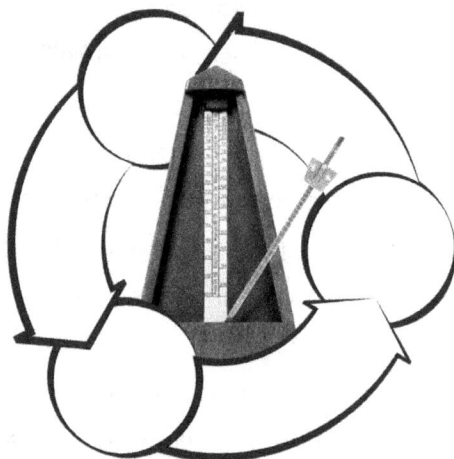

the objection is a benefit statement. Simply put a nod question on the end of that, "That's what you're really after, isn't it?" and you'll get your nod. And, your order. Or, in a worst case scenario, another objection so you can repeat the process and ask another nod question and close again.

Objections, to stay with the Nolan Ryan metaphor, are kind of like a hitter successfully fouling off Ryan's strikeout pitch. Ryan gets another shot.

But, that next pitch better not be in the same place as those thrown before it or the hitter—who is a big leaguer after all—will know it's coming and knock it out of the park.

For us, moving the ball around means having different closing questions to ask.

Closing Questions

I have always taught that there are three ways to close on that second or third nod.

1. **Direct Close**. The first closing question is a direct close. A direct close is a straightforward request for the business. It is a simple and short question using an economy of words and is designed to illicit a "Yes."

    "Can we go ahead and build the display?" "Is Tuesday OK for the first delivery?" "Do we have a deal?" "May I have your signature on this purchase order?" These are all examples. Short, to-the-point and straightforward requests for the business.

    If we get a "Yes," we're done. Get whatever detail you need taken care of and get out of there so you don't mess it up.

    If we get a "No," we're going to get an objection. No problem. We just circle it again to set up the next close. But, this second close won't work as well if it is the same exact close as the first one we just used. If you say, "Can we go ahead and build the display?" twice it is slightly pushy. But if you say "Can we go ahead and build the display?" a third time you are going to sound as if you are badgering the prospect. To avoid badgering your customer, use a different direct close or change to a different type of close. You could try the second kind of close: The choice close.

2. **Choice Close**. The choice close asks the buyer to choose between two alternative courses of action but each of them represents a "Yes."

   "Is morning or afternoon the best time for us to build it?"

   "Cash or charge?"

   "Do you want 100 units or will you need more than that?"

   The prospect is not given the choice of "Yes" or "No." Instead, the prospect is given the choice of "When?" or "How?" or "How Many?" I love choice closes because, frankly, I don't care which alternative the buyer picks because I got a "Yes" either way.

3. **Urgency Close**. If a choice close fails, then the third kind of close, the urgency close, is up next. With an urgency close, you give the buyer a reason to "not wait," to "not stall." If this sounds high pressure to you, think again. If this prospect truly has an unmet need and you truly have a feature/benefit relationship that will meet it, the question is not one of when, the question is one of "Yes" or "No."

So, your urgency close might sound like this, "Well, since we agree that you have this unmet need and we agree that this product or service meets it, can we go ahead today before we lose our place in production?" Or, "To get the check size up as soon as possible, may I put up the Point of Sale material tomorrow morning?" Or, "Well, there's no better time to start cutting fuel expense than right away. Can we set up the training for next week?"

An urgency close is logical once you have established that the unmet need urgently awaits satisfaction. There is no reason to wait. All this buyer needs is, with your help, to figure that out and it makes sense to decide now.

Of course, if the buyer says, "Let me think about it," that is referred to as a stall and defeating stalls is covered in Tool #10. If the buyer says, "Let me talk it over with others," that is referred to as a committee stall and, while also covered in Tool #10, the approach you take is different. Read more there.

[125

Point of Difference

Remember the power of the Points of Difference you bring to your prospect. It is with these PODs that you can most effectively close. Remind your prospect that only with you will they find these points of difference and the benefits they bring to satisfy the unmet need they possess. These logical points of difference are the very reasons why the prospect should say "Yes" to you.

WHAT I WOULD HAVE DONE DIFFERENTLY
IF I KNEW THEN WHAT I KNOW NOW

Not only would I have attempted to close much more quickly, I would have lost my fear of closing because I would have realized that the first "No" is not a bad thing (only a final "No" is bad). With the greater confidence that would have accrued to me, I'm certain I would have been much more successful. Nothing creates success like belief in success.

WHAT YOU SHOULD DO RIGHT NOW

Practice "The Circle" until you have the rhythm down.

1. You need BLANK (their unmet need)

2. Is that correct?

3. Get a Nod

4. I have BLANK (a feature)

5. Which gives you BLANK
    (a benefit that meets their unmet need)

6. Which is what you need, isn't it?

7. Get a Nod

8. Now, Close!

9. If your first close fails, circle back and
    close again using a different style

10. Repeat as needed until they are STUNned

Watch the ej4 video, "Closing the Sale," at STUNselling.com/closing
for more practice.

128]

TOOL #8

Overcoming Objections

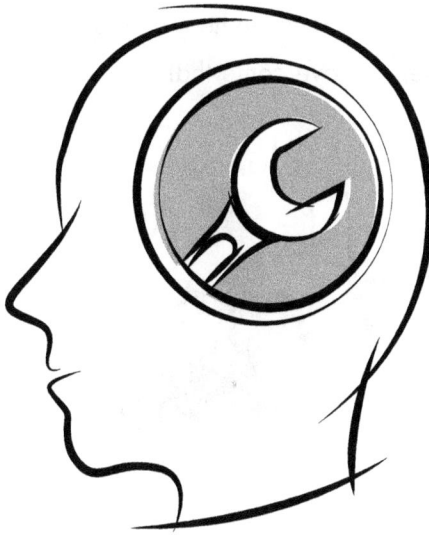

Here's What You're Going to Learn

There are four types of objections:

Misunderstanding, Doubt, Indifference and True Negative

For each type of objection, there is a unique way to address the customer's concern and turn his/her "No" into a "Yes" so you can close the sale.

THE POINT

Each type of objection must be resolved with a different approach in order to close the sale.

Real selling does not begin until we hear a "No" from the customer. Real selling happens when we overcome that "No" and turn it into a "Yes."

Huh-uh.
No. Nope.

That is what separates sellers from order takers. Each of us has heard countless objections in our time, but each of us has not thought about them from a theoretical perspective. Sure, we all understand the objection we hear over and over again about some feature of our product or service and, if we still have this sales job, we have figured out how to overcome that objection.

All sellers must look at objections from this more theoretical perspective. I have studied objections heard by sellers of beverages, financial services, advertising, baked goods, salty snacks, insurance, automotive aftermarket items, travel services and more. What I take away from all of this study and experience is that each and every objection I have ever heard in every industry I have ever worked can be categorized into one of four categories. Only four.

The categories are:

1. **Misunderstanding**
   the prospect misunderstands what we're saying

2. **Doubt**
   the prospect doesn't believe us

3. **Indifference**
   the prospect doesn't need what we're selling

4. **True Negative**
   there is something wrong with what we are selling

The reason I categorized objections for my clients is simple: As a sales training consultant, I needed to fully analyze each objection and strategize about how to overcome each one. It was through that process that I discovered every objection I've ever encountered fell into one of those four categories.

[131]

The important thing here is this: There is a very different process to follow to overcome a misunderstanding objection compared to, say, a true negative objection. Once again, each type of objection requires a different approach in order to close the sale.

The process for overcoming objections begins with us, as sellers, understanding the customer's unmet need, which is all part of sales psychology. Remember, as I first introduced in Tool #4, the psychology of the sale is a three step circle:

The customer needs something; we've got a product or service feature as a solution idea, which delivers a benefit, which satisfies the need. That circular relationship (You need this ▶ I've got this ▶ which can do that ▶ which is what you need) is the key to the sale. Especially important is the place where the benefit satisfies the need.

The thing that breaks up that circle is when the customer objects. When the customer objects, it's because they don't see the connection

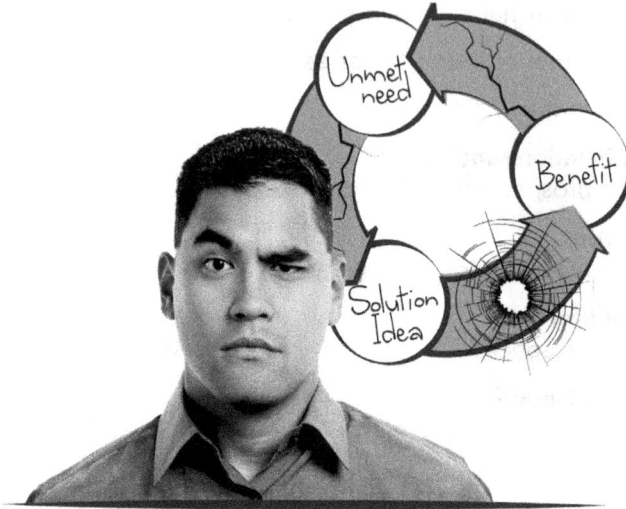

between your solution idea, the benefit and their unmet need. They don't think you're meeting their unmet need with your product or service. You have to begin with listening for the unmet need that their objection represents. You've got to cut through the clutter and set aside what you were going to say next. Instead, you must hear and fully understand what their unmet need is. Remember: "Without a need, don't proceed." Understanding where this person is coming from means understanding exactly what their unmet need is. Then, you must begin the process of empathizing with them. And, you must do this before you start offering up solutions.

It's important to express your empathy by saying something like, "Oh, yeah, I see what you mean, of course, I understand better now why you need that, I got it."

But, before you respond to the objection that they have just given to you, ask them: "Is there anything else?" "Is there anything else wrong?" "Is there anything else that's holding you back?"

It might sound something like this:

They say, *"OK, Mrs. Seller; I've heard what you've got to offer, but I need to tell you that your price is too high."*

You say, *"I see. You feel as if my price is too high. If I were in your shoes I would be very critical about price as well. I hear you. But, before I defend my price, let me ask you this: Is there anything else that concerns you—other than price?"*

Try to get them to tell you everything that's wrong, so you have all of their needs laid out. If they say, *"Well, as a matter of fact, yes. I am worried that you won't be able to deliver on time."*

You do the same thing you did with the price objection. *"Right. You're concerned not only with price, but also with timely delivery. That makes sense; it won't be of any use to you if it's late. I'll cover that too. Is there anything else?"*

About now, you're either going to get one more objection (*"You don't have exactly the right color I need"* or *"I heard that your product breaks down after a short period of time"* or *"I'm loyal to your competitor because she's my sister-in-law"* or whatever) or you're going to get this: *"No, that's it; I have no other concerns."*

[133

Now, like a successful cheater at cards, you've got a phenomenal and unfair advantage. When many sellers become discouraged, you can become empowered because you just got your counterpart to expose "their hand" all at once and in advance. You've yet to play a card and they've played all of theirs.

The magic moment has arrived: *"Of those objections, and they are all important and I'll cover each one, let me ask you where you want me to begin. In other words, which is most critical to you? Price? Delivery? Color? Which?"*

In essence, you're asking them to play their ace up front. Whatever they tell you next is their prime and most paramount unmet need—their most critical objection.

"Well, it's time-to-delivery."

Get them to prioritize their list for you.

STUN the most important first.

But, you must categorize that objection as to its type. And, remember, there are four types: Misunderstanding, Doubt, Indifference or True Negative. Then handle the objections, one by one, in the order of importance to them. I'll bet you this: After you've handled the most important one or two, the others will fade away and you'll close the deal before you even have to deal with them.

1. **Misunderstanding Objection**

   First among the types of objections is the misunderstanding objection. Misunderstandings occur when your customer just doesn't understand what you are saying. They think you are saying one thing when, actually, you are saying another. They don't know the real facts. They believe something else to be true.

   Misunderstanding objections can kill a sale and you'll never know what hit you. You defeat misunderstanding objections by first recognizing what is happening and then delivering a short, succinct and clear, clarifying straight answer followed by silence.

   Failing to recognize when a misunderstanding is occurring will kill the sale. Delivering a short clarification will save it.

   To overcome misunderstanding objections, give a straight answer, and then shut up.

   Oftentimes, as sales people, we tend to get carried away, jumping from benefits and solutions, and going through our standard pitches, so that we overload the customer with information – too much information so that what that person really needs to hear, the thing that satisfies their unmet need, gets lost in the mix. So, you give them a straight answer, and you follow that with silence. Give them a moment to understand or ponder what you just told them.

So, once again, if you identify the objection as a misunderstanding, offer a short, straight answer followed by absolute silence accompanied by a look of confidence. The silence part is critical. When you are silent, you have placed "the ball in their court." They have to talk next unless you let them off the hook by saying something. Be quiet. Let them process what you just said.

If they believe you, you will get a buying sign. Maybe it will sound like this. "Oh. I misunderstood. I thought blah blah blah. You're telling me that is not the case. OK. I see."

If their belief in the new truth is sincere, you close. "Well then, on that basis, do we have a deal?"

Of course, if they had another objection, rather than close, you might say something like: "OK. That's taken care of. Let's move to your second objection which was my price."

And you move forward to price. Price can either be a misunderstanding objection or a true negative objection. It is a misunderstanding objection if the truth is that you product or service isn't actually more expensive or that, over time, since yours lasts longer or works better, the higher up front price means a lower price when amortized over the life of the product.

If the latter is the case, you continue with the "straight answer and shut up" methodology:

> *"It is true that the upfront cost of my service is higher, but the monthly cost is lower. At the end of one year I'm not more expensive; I'm less expensive."*
> Then, silence.

If they believe you, you'll get a buying sign. A buying sign —an invitation to close— comes in the form of a nod of their head, a look of understanding or a comment such as, "Oh, I see. Good point." And, what do you do in response to a buying sign? You close, of course.

Misunderstandings occur when the buyer believes an untruth. When that happens, you say, "Oh, no, no, no I'm sorry, but I think you misunderstand."

"This product out-performs that product ten to one." (silence)

Or, "It'll work this time because of the innovations that we've incorporated." (silence)

Or, "No, no, studies show that this works better." (silence)

Or, "Actually, the truth is that you aren't positioned for maximum benefit right now." (silence)

When misunderstandings occur, your approach is to offer a straight answer followed by silence.

Well, then what happens? They either accept your answer, in which case you close because you've erased the misunderstanding. Or, they will reject your answer, in which case you find out why. If they reject your answer because they don't believe you, this objection has now become a doubt objection. Our process for those is different and will be covered next.

2. **Doubt Objection**

The second type of objection is the doubt objection. Doubt is when your customer doesn't believe what you're telling them. Either they think it's too good to be true, or they've heard something different somewhere else. If the objection is doubt, it's because they doubt the accuracy or the validity of what you say.

All customers, not just tough customers, will occasionally not believe what you tell them. They doubt the accuracy — or worse — the honesty of what you are saying.

"I don't believe that," when said by a customer will kill the sale. To defeat doubts, you need one and only one thing: Proof. Proof comes from a reliable outside source. Proof can be in the form of a customer testimonial, a research study or even an article from a trade journal. Without proof, doubts derail your success. "Trust me," doesn't work. Only actual proof beats doubt objections. The way you handle a doubt objection is simple. Provide proof. Proof is a powerful thing especially when followed by silence.

[137

When they say, "I don't believe you," you can't just say, "Trust me." That doesn't work. You can't say, "Uhhhh, can I get back to you on that?" That won't work either. To overcome the doubt objection, you have to have proof right then. If you don't currently have a proof source for the doubt objections you are hearing, get with your boss, your coworkers, the other people in your company, and ask for assistance. The marketing people should step up here. Their job is to go get those proofs.

Ideally you will know this is a possible objection before the meeting, and will come armed with proof sources in anticipation. They will only accept your solution when you can PROVE your solution. And they will reject your solution when you can't.

Proof comes in all kinds of forms: It comes as information, like data and numbers. It comes in pictures — a picture is worth a thousand words, and worth a thousand pieces of data. Testimonials from a satisfied customer who has the same unmet need counts as a proof source. A similar situation you can cite where someone else had a relatable unmet need, implemented your solution, and had successful results is a proof source. These are called proof sources because they are more than an assurance from you; they count as hard evidence proving the value, quality, durability, ability to satisfy the unmet need.

As you're giving your proof, listen and watch for a buying sign. If they nod, or say "I see what you mean," those are buying signs. If they say "Oh!" that's a buying sign. You close on buying signs.

During presentations and speeches, whenever the subject of marketing came up — and it came up a lot — and I was asked about the difference was between sales people and marketing people, I would always say that marketing people are just like sales people except they can't close. Further truth of this difference is this: Sales people need the marketing people to provide them with proofs for doubt objections so they can close.

"Trust me!" No way. Why should they trust you? They'll trust an unbiased outsider, a third party with no reason to lie or stretch the truth; but not you. "Hey, would I lie to you?" They may not say it but, often, their answer would be "Yes. You're a sales person and sales people will lie to get a sale." And, of course, sadly, many do.

In the soft drink business, in high market share areas, we would always talk about market share to secure additional space on the shelf and on display. Our competition would talk about market share as well. The customer would tell us that our share numbers didn't match. For example, when my friends at Coca-Cola would talk about market share in a particular market, they would always discuss total share which includes fountain drinks. Since McDonald's and Wendy's and Burger King all sold thousands of gallons of Coke, Coke's overall share would invariably be much higher than Pepsi's. However, in many markets, in the grocery channel where there was little or no fountain business to include in the calculations, Pepsi would have a higher share than Coke. So, in those markets, Pepsi would cite take home or packaged beverage shares. The customer was confused.

[139

Two things were happening. First, there was a misunderstanding. "The Coke guy says they have a higher share and you say Pepsi has a higher share. I don't trust either one of you."

"I hear you, Mr. Customer. If I were you and I was hearing inconsistent information I wouldn't trust either one of us either. But, the truth of the matter is that Pepsi's share is higher IN YOUR CHANNEL. When you take out the fountain drinks sold at fast food restaurants where the consumer has no choice because only one cola is for sale and look at share data in your channel — the grocery channel — where consumers always have a choice, Pepsi's share is higher. I can prove it. Look at these numbers from Neilsen. See? Here at the top, it says: 'Grocery Channel.' Now, look at these numbers, also from Neilsen. See? Here is says, 'All channels.' You don't care about all channels because you're not in all channels, you're in the grocery channel where consumers have a choice. Isn't that true?" (That's a nod question.)

"Don't believe me and don't believe my competition. Believe Neilsen. They've not only got no reason to lie but they would be out of business if they did. Isn't that also true?" (Another nod question.)

That was Proof. It came from an unbiased outside source: Neilsen.

I once did some sales consulting and training for Macklanburg-Duncan where I learned a lot about caulk. I originally thought that all caulk was the same. So did a considerable number of hardware and home store buyers. But M-D had great scientific literature showing test after test where their high end caulk was better than their competitor's high end caulk. That literature counted as a proof source. [Note: In 2000, Macklanburg-Duncan divested its caulk and sealant business to GE.]

It was the same when I consulted with Pennzoil. They had a veritable fountain of lab produced proof sources to back up their claims. Syngenta (the seed company) had volumes of yield tests from fields across the farm belt and each served as a prime proof source.

Auto manufacturers like to cite car magazines and consumer products companies are always trying to find a legal way to make use of *Consumer Reports* research data. Why? Because people believe *Car and Driver* and *Consumer Reports* but they don't believe the car salespeople. The car sellers need proof and, when that proof comes from *Road and Track Magazine*, it matters.

Angie's List and Yelp and TripAdvisor are internet proof vehicles that prospective buyers of home services or lodging can use as a proof source for the claims made on vendor web sites.

If you don't already have proof for the claims you make, go find proof. You'll need it. The first place to look is to the Marketing Department. That's a big part of their job.

3. **Indifference Objection**

The third type of objection is the indifference objection. Of the four types of objections, the most difficult to overcome is indifference. The indifferent customer rejects the premise of your existence: That he or she possesses an unmet need. Without a need, don't proceed. How do you overcome the indifference objection? You stop selling and return to the unmet need. Once the customers' unmet need is acknowledged, indifference becomes interest. When it comes to indifference, "I don't need it," is a fatal illness. "Yes, you do," is the cure.

[141]

The first step to beating this most difficult of objections is to understand what the unmet need is. Customers have an unmet need, we're selling something that delivers some sort of a benefit which has got to satisfy the need. So it makes a circle. "Mr. Customer, you need this, I've got this, which gives you that, which solves your need."

Now, when your customer says, "I don't think so", it's because they've got an objection. They are rejecting your solution because it doesn't meet (or they don't think it meets) their need. Or, in the case of indifference objections, they reject the notion that they have the need upon which you are basing your sales presentation. You've got to understand the unmet need before you can begin presenting a solution and they've got to acknowledge the need before it matters to them. Without that, you're not going anywhere together.

The indifference objection is the one that drives me crazy. The hardest customer to sell to in the world is the one that doesn't need what you've got. Indifference objections mean, very simply, that we got the need wrong because they don't see the benefit as something they want. We don't really understand the customer's unmet need. And we're going to have to ask more questions to figure out what the real unmet need is.

While this book is about selling, I use the indifference objection most frequently when I am buying. Let's use automobiles as an example. When I am ready to buy a new car I am at the mercy of the new car salesperson because I think I need a new car. The salesperson knows that because I just walked onto their lot. It's too easy for them. So, I always pretended that I didn't need a new car at all; that I was just killing time. Then I would say, "But, since I am here, if you can convince me that I need something new, I guess I could trade."

Then, no matter what they showed me, I found some reason why that was not the vehicle I needed. After a half hour of that, they would become very frustrated. That's what I wanted. I would then sum up, "Of everything that you've shown me, the only one — the only one — that would maybe be something I could own was that red one." You know what happened next? They started aggressively talking price. I loved that. It just set me up to offer more objections!

As a seller, the question to which you need an answer is this: "Ultimately what do you really want this thing to do for you?"

Start really drilling into the need; get it into the overall picture. Remember that you aren't selling a product or service. You are selling the benefit your customer receives when they buy your product of service. And, for that benefit to matter, it must satisfy an unmet need that your customer has in the forefront of his mind. Without that need, you are going to have an indifferent customer. So, without a need, don't proceed.

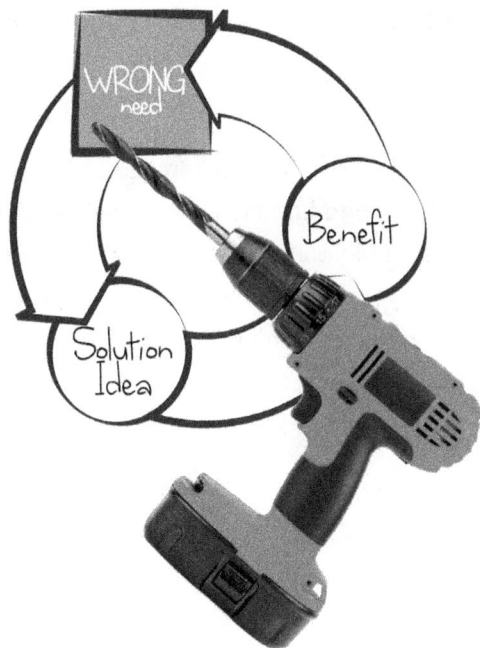

"What final results are you actually after?" "What aren't you getting from your current supplier?" "What goals are not being met?" Don't talk about your product or service until you talk about these other things; these unmet needs.

Once the customer gives you the answer, speak back their need to them to make sure you understand it. They'll either accept that or they won't. If they reject what you've said, well, that means you did not find the REAL unmet need. The key to the sale is the unmet need. When you can satisfy the real unmet need, the customer can no longer be indifferent. Then you can STUN them.

So, if you get the indifference objection, go back to the need. Listen, and watch for buying signs. If you blew the need the first time around and you get it the second time, you'll see it because the customer nods. When that happens, then you work the rest of the circle. If the prospect is agreeing with the need that you have restated to him and agreeing that you have shown how your product or service delivers a benefit that satisfies that need, he'll say, "Ah, I see what you mean, that would help me." That's a buying sign. Close on buying signs. Never miss a buying sign, always close.

What's the answer to the indifference objection? Find the right need. Go back and find the REAL unmet need. He doesn't need another facing of your product, but he does need the extra money the facing of your product would give him. And remember, always talk benefits, don't talk so much about the solution idea, talk more about the benefits, the money, that that idea will deliver. And you'll get that indifference objection to go away.

In the Budweiser world, A-B sales folks would constantly try to sell bar owners on the idea of putting in a keg of Bud in place of that existing keg of a different brand. The old fancy tap handle would get unscrewed and set aside and a new fancy tap handle would go up in its place. Or, at least that was the idea. But often the bar owner would simply say that he felt that he didn't need Budweiser on draught because he already had it in bottles. He had no need to switch out that tap handle.

The salesperson had to stop selling the idea of the Bud handle and start selling the idea of getting more consumers to buy a draught beer because the brand they preferred was available on tap. Since the bar's penny profit on a glass of beer was greater than their penny profit on a bottle of beer, the salesperson was, in essence, telling the bar owner that cannibalizing his bottle sales a bit and increasing his draft sales a bit was a good move when one looked at the bottom line.

In that bar, selling the beer wasn't the best idea. In that bar, selling the idea that the beer would bring in more beer drinkers or cause beer drinkers to come in more frequently or cause beer drinkers to buy "just one more draught" made sense. That's because the bar owner didn't need the beer. What he really needed was more traffic, more repeat traffic or more drinks per customer. Of course, this all had to be done within reason when the product was beer. If the bar owner sold the consumer too much beer that was a bad thing. The good thing was to have more people buying the right amount of beer. It was tricky and a quite a few beer sellers never got the hang of it.

In the snack cake business, the convenience store owner didn't need a rack of Dolly Madison snack cakes. What the store needed was an impulse item that consumers would pick up from an appropriately placed rack so as to drive up the average transaction size.

In the soft drink business, the fast food operator didn't need Mountain Dew. What he needed was a brand of soft drink that would cause water drinkers to <u>buy</u> a beverage instead of not buying a beverage. What he needed was a consumer who would buy a large instead of a small drink. What he needed was revenue. He didn't need the brand. He needed the benefit it would bring.

[145

Indifferent customers are simply not focused on the need they have. If they're not focused on their unmet need, it is the seller's job to get them focused.

"I get that you don't need Mountain Dew. What you need is a brand that these young guys want to buy in a large cup. Would you agree with that?"

"I understand that you don't need a snack cake rack. What you need is something to drive up your average transaction size. That's true, isn't it?"

Once you've got the nod to the question that confirms the need, you can go back to your Circle. You can't STUN without the UN.

"Well, I've got Mountain Dew. It sells larger sizes to the young male demographic. That means they spend more money with you. That's what you want, isn't it?"

"Uh, yes. That's what I want."

"May I switch your fountain unit over?" Silence.

"Well, I've got a beautiful cake rack that will fit right here, right next to the register. When people are in line to pay for their gas, they'll pick up some Dunkin' Sticks™ which means your transaction size will go up. That's what you want, isn't it?"

"Uh, yes. That's important to me."

"May I bring in the rack?"

Sometimes, customers are indifferent for another reason. That is when they acknowledge their need but don't acknowledge that it is unmet. They need something but their current supplier is already satisfying that need. Their need is not unmet, so they are indifferent to your offer. When that happens, imagine that you have a kids' playground teeter-totter in front of you. Your customer has placed your competitor's offering on one side of the teeter-totter and you are sitting on the other side. You don't outweigh your competitor so the teeter-totter doesn't tip your way.

Start piling the benefits of your product on your side. When you see it start to tip in your direction, this kind of indifference is going away. The trick here is to always remember that you can't pile product or service features onto the teeter-totter. You can only pile benefits there. And, those benefits won't tip the scale unless they satisfy a primary unmet need of your prospect — in this case they've got to satisfy it better than your competitor already is satisfying it.

When it tips, close. You can tell when it tips if you watch their head. When they nod or when they change their facial expression to one of grudging acceptance, that's a buying sign. That's the tipping happening right before your eyes. It is your cue to close.

4. **True Negative Objection**

The fourth and final type of objection is the true negative objection. It occurs all the time. Your product or service isn't perfect; somewhere there is a flaw in what you are offering. That flaw need not be fatal. The flaw must first be acknowledged. Quickly thereafter, it must be overwhelmed by benefits.

[147

True negatives are overcome by benefits. Imagine the negatives sitting on one side of a scale and benefits sitting on the other side. The scale tips when the benefits have more weight than the true negative does.

To describe true negatives, think about this: What do you do when the customer says, "Your competitor's got something better." If it isn't true, you deal with it as you would any misunderstanding objection. You give a straight answer that says, in essence, that you're better. If they don't believe you, you deal with it as you would any doubt objection. You provide proof. But, what do you do when it is true; when your competitor's offering is better?

Ah, a true negative objection. Remember, real selling doesn't begin until you get the first "No." You've got to turn that "No" into a "Yes." And not all "No's" can be turned into "Yes's" in the same way. This is particularly true with true negative objections.

When your customer presents a true negative objection and points out there is something that's really wrong with, or less good, about your solution, and they are correct, you may as well just agree. Don't try and tap dance your way through it. Just say, "You know what, you're right. On this point, you're correct. Mine is not as good as the other guy's. But on all the other points, mine is better. Your job as the buyer is to figure out which of our solutions is best when all the variables are taken into consideration rather than just one or two."

Here's the key with the true negative: You've got to outweigh, with benefits, your competition. You've got to outweigh this true negative with a whole bunch of positives.

This one negative won't mess up the sale because all of these other positives you've got to outweigh it. So you outweigh the true negatives with benefits illustrated with benefit statements.

We're back to our teeter-totter.

The competition has one benefit on one side and the lever is tipped in their favor. You need to put two benefits on your side to tip it back in your favor. One benefit on their side that you can't match doesn't spoil the deal.

"True, our price is higher, but you end up making more money because our resale margin is higher."

"True, our product doesn't fix as many problems as that guy's does, but the extra problems that other guy fixes don't occur as often. Ours fixes the big problems that occur most often. Those are the ones you really care about."

"True, this one costs more when you buy it, but it costs less to operate, less to maintain, it lasts longer, so it costs you less over the long-haul."

Give them the truth; give them the true main point.

"True, our delivery date is farther out, but when it does get here, it'll fix more problems. The quick fix won't fix all the problems. Ours will fix all the problems. For the best solution, you need to wait."

[149

If they reject your answer, it means you didn't have enough benefits to tip the scale far enough for them to say "Yes". Go find some more benefits. When they accept your answer – close. True negatives are the easiest objections there are if you truly understand all of the benefits you have to offer and how each one matches up with the unmet need of this particular buyer.

So, there you have it, the four objections: Misunderstanding, Doubt, Indifference and True Negative. Don't forget: Real selling does not begin until you hear "No." If you get all the objections out, you'll get to the "Yes" that much more quickly. So learn to categorize and then prioritize the objections, and go to the most important first and use the appropriate approach. If you then listen and watch for buying signs from that customer, whenever they begin to accept your answer, then it's done, stop. Close on that buying sign. Close on it right then.

WHAT I WOULD HAVE DONE DIFFERENTLY
IF I KNEW THEN WHAT I KNOW NOW

I would have talked a lot less and I would have been much more relaxed. While I once dreaded objections of any sort, I would have sought them out instead. And, my selling would have happened in much less time. Instead of meticulously covering each and every feature and listing benefit after benefit, I would have used The Circle and closed quickly to flush out objections.

"Mrs. Prospect, you need this. I've got this for you. It will do this for you which satisfies your need. That's what you want, isn't it?" To that, if I've circled correctly, I'll get this reply, "Yes. That is what I need."

Then I would close. "So, can I set that up for you right away?" Then I would have used deafening silence to place the ball squarely in the customer's court – it would have allowed them time to digest the opportunity and then they would have been required to make a decision.

I would have either gotten a "Yes" or, more likely, "Whoa. Wait a minute. I've got a couple of concerns about this." Then I would have said, "Great. Let's talk about those concerns."

Objections would flow. As each one was revealed, I would ask if there were others. I would empathize with each one along the way. After the final objection was revealed, I would have sought to arrange

THEN... CONTINUED

them from most important to least important by asking, "Which of those is most critical for you? Where would you like me to begin?"

It would have been great fun. Instead of dreading objections, I would have sought them out. Instead of arguing with my prospect, I would have been reasoning with my prospect. And, most certainly, I would have been not only more successful, I would have been happier.

[151

Had the objection been one of...

- MISUNDERSTANDING... I would have given a straight answer followed by silence. If the truth of my answer was accepted, I would close.

- DOUBT... I would have had evidence to back up my claims. I would have collected testimonials from high school principals and yearbook advisors attesting to the veracity of my assertions. I would have had similar testimonials from college kids who were formerly on the yearbook staff in high school talking briefly about how what they learned from me made them more successful in college or helped them choose a major there.

THEN... CONTINUED

- INDIFFERENCE... I would have had an answer for all those schools that told me they were happy with their current supplier; that they had no reason to change. Sure, my book and the book my competitor would deliver might not, in the end, be that different. Sure, my services cost more than the Walsworth guy was charging. But, those things didn't matter.

    - "You want that book here on the day it's promised, is that correct?" ▶ "Yes."

    - "You want that book delivered on or under budget, is that correct?" ▶ "Yes."

    - "You want that book to contain no embarrassing surprises for this school. Is that correct?" ▶ "Absolutely."

    - "Well, that's what I'm selling. On time, on budget, no surprises, no embarrassment. That's what you want, isn't it." ▶ "Sure is."

      ▶ "With those as my guarantees, will you switch?" Silence.

THEN... CONTINUED

■ TRUE NEGATIVE... I would not have been afraid to discuss where my shortcomings were. In the case of my yearbook sales career, my major true negative objection was price. We were the highest price. Because I was afraid to tell them my price, I couldn't close. Because I couldn't close, I couldn't succeed. Were I back there today I would begin with price.

[153

"Mrs. High School Principal, let me make one thing clear right at the onset. It will cost you more to deal with me than it is costing you to deal with your current publisher. When you see all that you receive for that higher price, you'll be happy to pay it." Then? Onto the benefits; particularly the benefits that best satisfied the principal's most important or most urgent unmet need.

WHAT YOU SHOULD DO RIGHT NOW

Write down the top five or ten objections you hear on a regular basis. Look at each one closely. Categorize them among the four types of objections: Misunderstanding, Doubt, Indifference, True Negative.

For those that are Misunderstanding Objections, are any of these situations where the customer believes the truth to be one thing when it is actually another? If one or more of your frequent objections is a misunderstanding, write down what the shortest possible straight answer is that would help them to understand. Then go back and see if you can shorten that answer even more.

For those that are Doubt Objections, where, in essence, the customer is saying, "I don't buy that" or "I don't believe you?" For those objections, getting down on one knee and saying in your most sincere voice the words, "Trust me. Would I lie to you?" simply isn't good enough. Get with your sales manager or go directly to marketing and get proof. Go to your current or former customers and get them to give you testimonials which back up the veracity of your claims. Get proof. Remember, the best proof comes from an unbiased third party.

NOW... CONTINUED

For those that are Indifference Objections, figure out what your prospect's real unmet need is. Is it customer traffic? Is it budgetary? Is it quality? Is it increased transaction size? Whenever that prospect is indifferent to your product or service, start selling traffic or budget or quality or transaction size. The indifference will vanish. Why? Because that's what he needs.

For those that are True Negative Objections, quit worrying about your shortcomings. Nobody's perfect. Draw a teeter-totter diagram on a piece of paper. Put the biggest true negative that comes with your product or service on one side. Now, put the benefits you offer on the other side. In your mind's eye, you'll know when those benefits outweigh the true negative. When you see that, you no longer have anything to fear.

Confirm your understanding of the four types of Objections by watching the ej4 videos on the topic at STUNselling.com/objections.

TOOL #9

Handling Tough Customers

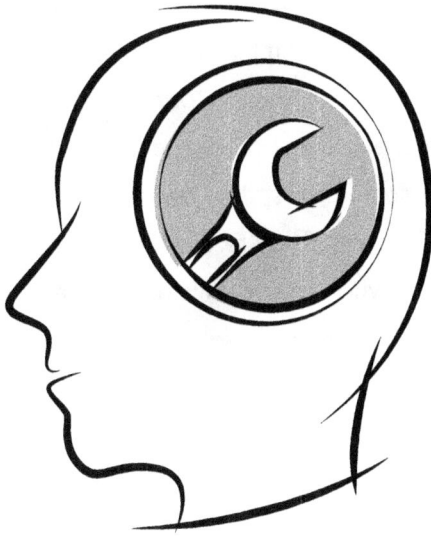

Here's What You're Going to Learn

Tough customers can be sold.

In fact, they are the most fun to sell to once you figure out how to do it. What you do is simple really. You pound on their unmet need until they cede the point. Then, you move forward, cautiously, with features and benefits that relate to the unmet need they are willing to acknowledge.

THE POINT

We all love the easy customers. They believe what we tell them. They nod vigorously when we nail a benefit statement. In some cases, they are actually pulling for us to win. On the other side of the customer coin, we all become apprehensive about the other ones — the tough customers. Tough customers don't answer our questions completely or forthrightly preferring to hide critical information from us. They don't give an inch when we make a good point, never rewarding us with a nod as a buying sign. In some cases, they are friends with our competition. They are, in a word, tough. They're the ones that keep us up at night. They are also the ones who test our skills and make us better. Though we don't learn much when we make a sale, we should learn volumes when we fail to make a sale.

At Helzberg Diamonds, I learned about a customer process that I had never before experienced called "T.O." T.O. is an acronym for "turn over"—essentially, one associate may strategically decide to turn over a customer to another associate so that the team is doing the selling rather than one individual doing the selling.

In their retail jewelry stores, Helzberg people "turn over" a tough customer to another Helzberg person. This process works because they have institutionalized a methodology whereby when one salesperson is failing to move the sale forward, a second salesperson always enters the picture and takes over the lead. Sometimes, the original seller withdraws a just a little — sometimes completely — depending on the reaction of the prospect.

Part of the reason that this works for them so well comes back, I believe, to personality types. When the customer and the seller don't mesh and the dynamic between them is less than perfect, Helzberg substitutes a different seller who, naturally, uses their unique personality to better communicate the perfect match between the product and the customer's need for the product. A critical learning point here is that the unmet need, the product (or service) being offered and the benefit of that product (or service) does not change. The thing that changes is the way the psychological circle is addressed.

I heard of one situation where four different Helzberg people turned a tough customer over until, finally, one of them was successful in closing the sale. Neither the product nor the price at which it was offered changed along the way. What changed was the person delivering the message.

[159

Arguably, a single person might be able to internally turn over this tough customer. By that I mean if one approach taken by, say, a High D salesperson fails to work, that same salesperson could "put on a mask" and adjust to a different approach — maybe that of a High S — and find that now the sale can progress as a result of having taken a different personality-driven approach to the sale.

However, from the customer's perspective, this may be unrealistic or impossible. If the customer notes that the seller is changing personality, they may rightly feel as though they were somehow being manipulated by an unscrupulous sales person. However, when a new seller enters the picture and the former seller subtly backs away, a new approach feels more natural and in no way manipulative.

In many businesses, this would be an unlikely scenario because of the selfish nature of the sellers involved. When one seller backs away, they would be giving up their commission while simultaneously admitting defeat — two things sellers are loathe to do. However, a sales team leader must ask whether or not it is more important for one specific salesperson to succeed at satisfying the customer's unmet need vs. the enterprise succeeding at doing the same.

Helzberg's solution is to minimize selfishness by sharing the commission and heaping appreciation and recognition on the seller who was wise enough to back away when he or she realized that they were failing to succeed with this "tough customer."

While it is true that tough customers are tough with all of us, they are undoubtedly much tougher with those of us who are unwilling or unable to adjust our approach — our personality style — during the execution of the all-important psychological circle of selling. "When at first you don't succeed, let somebody else try again," is the mantra at Helzberg. The results don't lie: The enterprise is much more successful because it adopts this stance. Now, I am going to oversimplify. Tough customers become much more reasonable if you always remember to use the psychological circle when you prepare for them, when you present to them and when you are overcoming their objections. It doesn't make sense for any customer to reject acknowledgement of a real unmet need that they have. It doesn't make sense for them to reject a benefit that clearly satisfies an unmet need turning it into a met need. If you're good at turning features into benefits, it doesn't make sense for them to reject that process either.

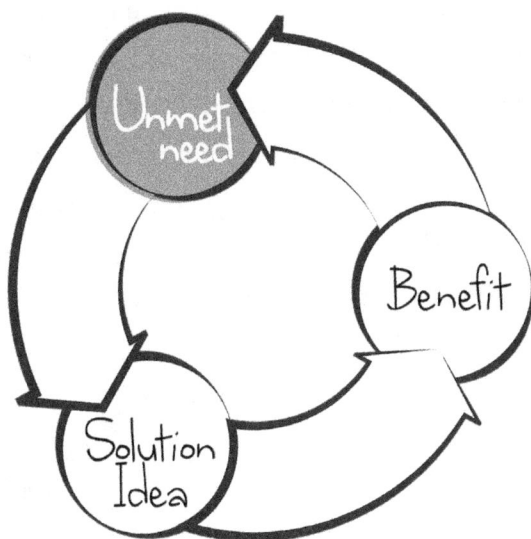

What does that leave? It leaves very few logical reasons for them to continue to be considered "tough." They may, however, revert to illogical reasons and, unfortunately, you need to prepare for that eventuality. We're going to refer to this concept as *reasonable* and *unreasonable* unmet needs. Neither of these has anything to do with you as a seller. They have everything to do with your customer as a buyer. Said another way, they will throw these *reasonable* and *unreasonable* unmet needs at anyone and everyone who comes to sell something to them. Don't think that you're alone in calling them tough customers because you're not. While I don't encourage you to go and meet with your competitor, I will predict that should you ever do that, you will both agree about these people. They are tough with everybody; not just you.

Here are some examples of unreasonable unmet needs. They're having a bad day. They've got a sick significant other. Their kid is in trouble at school or with the law. They've got a problem with another supplier and they are taking it out on you. The IRS has just informed them of an audit of their income taxes from three years ago. Maybe they've got a rock in their shoe. Indeed, they're having a bad day and they need a way to make it a good day and they have a perverted sense that if they make your day bad theirs will improve.

These are all examples of unreasonable unmet needs. You can't satisfy these needs. You can't be blamed because they exist. You shouldn't have to deal with them or with this person when they are fixated on them. You, my friend, are in the right place at the wrong time. I am sorry.

To be sure, there are reasonable causes for them to be tough. Maybe your product or service standards are too low to satisfy their needs. Maybe your organization delivered subpar service in the past. Maybe your company was late with a delivery or provided them with an inaccurate invoice. Perhaps, in the recent or distant past, you or your predecessor committed an error or really let them down.

Earlier in this section you found Tool #5 describing the four personality types that you will find in the customers upon whom you call. Two of those tend to be tough: Dominant personality types (High D) and compliant personality types (High C). Statistically, those two groups make up about a third of the population. Extrapolating that, you should expect — if you are average — to find that one third of your customers are tough. If your organization is exemplary that number will be lower. If your organization has a poor track record, that number will be much higher. You, fairly or unfairly, are stuck with the past and with the performance of others over whom you had or have little or no control.

Consider these tips when dealing with tough customers:

- **Tough customers sometimes yell**.
  When they do, lower your volume. Never try to keep up with or out shout them. That is a losing proposition.

- **Too much detail results in more aggravation**.
  Tough customers are looking for anything they can find to be tough about. Give them as little as possible with which to find fault. Refrain from providing them with details that are not required to prove that your feature/benefit relationship satisfies their unmet need.

- **Keep your sentences short; get to the point**.
  If they ask a question, don't vacillate. Give them a short answer that is definite. Give them proof sources when there is a doubt. Offer guarantees when you can. Never make an excuse for a service or product failure. Instead, acknowledge it and provide reasons why that will not recur. Provide testimonials. Never argue without the facts at your fingertips. If you have facts, argue back just a little. They will respect you for it. But, keep your cool while you argue. Remember to never argue emotionally; only factually with proof sources at the ready. Acknowledge and absorb fault even when the real blame lies with others. Simply say, "I will personally see to it that never happens again." Passing the buck with this customer means you'll never earn any bucks from this customer.

[163

- **Tolerate conflict.**
Tough customers love conflict. The way you handle conflict will determine how they evaluate you. If you don't handle conflict well, they will brand you as weak and incompetent. How do you handle conflict? Don't react.

Keep cool. Stay focused on our circle beginning with their unmet need because that is your only route to success.

- **Do not become the old time stereotypical "salesman."**
Don't tell the joke. Don't make inane comments about the weather. Don't ask about their family or try to relate with them about their hobby. Focus with laser-like concentration on their primary and most urgent unmet business need. Do not allow them to divert you from that; they will try.

- **Stay calm**. Tough customers enjoy rattling salespeople. Ask about their unmet need. Use silence and listen to their unmet need. Don't ever cut them off. Let them vent.

Apologize for failures. Empathize with their plight. Repeat back what they told you to confirm that you have real understanding. Offer a solution that delivers benefits that satisfy their unmet need. If you can, offer more than one to provide them with a choice. Choose the best solution idea and implement it.

■ **Follow-up with this customer is critical**.
Your solution must work; it must do what you said it would do and it must satisfy their unmet need or they are going to be tougher than ever. Never over-promise and under-deliver. The reverse of that is most wise with a tough customer.

■ **Be prepared to walk away** so you can live to "fight" another day. If this person is truly having the worst day of their life, you aren't going to fix it. All you're going to do is provide them with somebody to beat on. Get out of there. Don't burn your bridge on the way out.

■ **Turn over this tough customer to another member of your team**.
Because a colleague may take a different approach to the psychological circle, he/she may be more successful in closing the sale.

■ **Silence is a great response to tough customers**.
Never interrupt them no matter how long they want to rail. Listen for the unmet need. Find the benefit you can actually deliver that will satisfy that unmet need.

That's how you make the tough customer less tough.

WHAT I WOULD HAVE DONE DIFFERENTLY
IF I KNEW THEN WHAT I KNOW NOW

I would have talked less and listened more. I would have empathized more. I would have taken all the blame for failures on my own shoulders and never finger-pointed. I would have used an economy of words and volunteered less information, particularly potentially irrelevant facts.

Most importantly, I would never have taken these types of customers personally. Today I understand that tough customers are tough with every seller—not just with me. That means that I am not the problem. In fact, if I can uncover and understand their true unmet need, I am the solution.

With tough customers, the circle is the key. They need this. You've got that. It does this and that's what they need. Silence.

WHAT YOU SHOULD DO RIGHT NOW

Think about and write down the true business unmet needs of every customer that you can reasonably label as being tough. Then, write down the feature/benefit relationships that you can discuss from one of the products or services that you have on offer for this customer. Practice saying the circle in as few words as possible.

[167

Reach down deep inside and find the strength to never fight back because whoever angers you, controls you. And you can't let this person do that to you. Stay cool, my friend. Think about the poor slob who is going to follow you into this tough customer's office. Think about the fact that they may not have read this book and they are a lamb headed for slaughter. Rejoice in the fact that it's not you that's at issue.

Easier said — or written — than done. But, doable none the less.

Bolster your confidence by watching this short video, "Handling Tough Customers," located at STUNselling.com/tough_customers.

TOOL # 10

Defeating Stalls

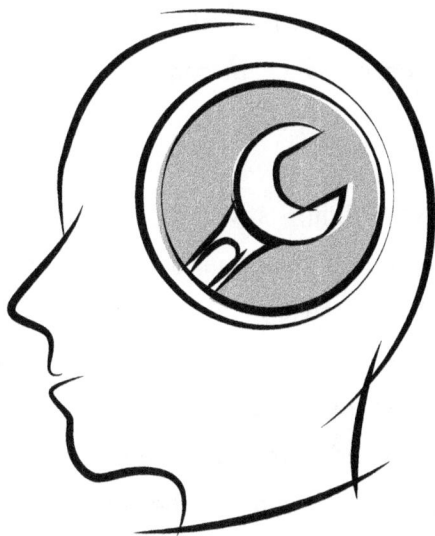

Here's What You're Going to Learn

Most sales professionals are all too familiar with buyers who, rather than making a yes/no decision, simply stall.

There are two different types of stalls. The first is the easiest to defeat: "Let me think about it." The second is harder: "I'll have to talk to someone else before I can give you an answer." This second type of stall has been typically referred to as the "Committee Stall" because bankers use it all the time when talking to a prospective borrower. The banker wants to be the borrower's friend so they never say "No." They simply tell the borrower that they don't have the decision making authority required so they have to take the matter to "The Loan Committee." Hence: "The Committee Stall." This one can be defeated too; it's just tougher and requires pre-planning.

THE POINT

A stall is neither a "Yes" nor a "No." The problem is that when a stall is accepted, it seldom becomes a "Yes" and often dissolves into a "No."

"The customer is always right," is wrong. With apologies to whomever first said it (Harry Gordon Selfridge, John Wanamaker or Marshall Field), I don't buy it. As a seller, I believe that when a customer stalls they are abdicating their responsibility to make a decision that is in the best interests of their enterprise. They aren't earning their money as a buyer. They aren't prepared or they aren't brave or they aren't confident of their ability to do the right thing. So, they do nothing. Doing nothing, when you're a buyer, is usually not the right thing.

Customers who stall should either be saying "Yes," or saying "No." Saying, "Let me think about it," or stalling, is tantamount to saying, "I don't know what to do so I am going to do nothing instead."

Of course, it could be our fault that the customer isn't making a decision. Maybe we didn't uncover the correct or most urgent unmet need they have. Maybe our feature-benefit explanation didn't make sense to them. Maybe our benefit didn't clearly satisfy their unmet need and turn it into a met need. Maybe they misunderstood. Maybe our competitor has something better. Maybe they don't believe our claims. Maybe it is more than one of these things.

But, if it is one or more of those things, that's a reason to say, "No." It is not a reason to say, "Let me think about it." To me, this is particularly true when, in my personal experience and in the personal experience of the literally thousands of sellers I have surveyed on this point, almost never does the buyer actually go and think about it. During hundreds of training sessions, I have asked for a show of hands to this question: "How many of you have ever had a buyer who said, 'Let me think about it,' call you up a few days later and say, 'I thought about it and the answer is, 'Yes.''" I've never gotten a hand raised in response to that question.

In fact, when I continue to survey, "How many of you have heard a buyer say this when you asked them during a follow-up call, 'Did you think about it?' say, 'Uh, well, no, uh, I haven't had time.'" I get lots of hands on that one.

Come on, buyers. Give us a "Yes" or give us a "No" but don't give us a "Let me think about it." That's nothing more—most often—than a "No" you're saving for later. Do you as buyers understand the stress and angst that puts on us sellers? We think that maybe you're going to say "Yes" after you think about it but we almost never do. We sellers go back to our bosses and they ask us, "Well, what happened?" We try to put on our best face and say something like, "She was really receptive.

When I asked her if she had any concerns going forward, she said 'No.' She said that she just needed some time to think about it. I'm pretty sure that there is nothing that is going to make her say, 'No.' So, I'd say that the chances we're going to get this are pretty good."

We just told our boss that the answer is probably going to be "Yes," but that it will happen a bit later on. Taking us at our word, the boss puts that in the status column as "highly probable." Our boss tells her boss that we probably have the deal. Her boss puts it in the "sold next week" column. Everybody thinks this has a much greater chance of really happening that it really does. When, after a week or two, we go back and the buyer gives us the bad news or simply re-stalls, we are not only disappointed, we must now go back and tell our superiors that we didn't get the deal they thought we had already probably gotten.

I hate stalls. Hate 'em. And, I try to never ever use the word "hate." I don't care for it. It is too polarizing and too negative. But, I do hate stalls.

Actually, there are two kinds of stalls and I hate them both. One is the buyer not being a very good buyer who was just pitched by a seller who may not have been a very good seller. That's the "Think About It Stall."

The second kind of stall happens when the buyer says, "Let me talk it over with my spouse," or, "Let me talk it over with my team," or, "Let me take it to the committee." That one is called the "Committee Stall" and when it happens, we would have seen it coming had we done our homework. We should have anticipated all committee stalls.

It is going to be important from here onward that we use these labels: "Think About It Stall" and "Committee Stall." The labels themselves aren't critical. What's critical is to know what we must do in response to each of these two different events. Both are stalls but they bear no resemblance to each other beyond that simple fact.

[173

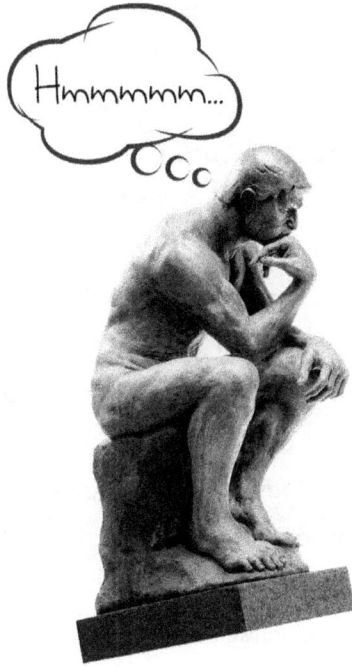

Let Me Think About It Stall

When you hear the words, "Let me think about it," you need to do something to keep this process going right now. If you leave, the buyer isn't going to clear his/her desk and begin to think about anything you just proposed. No. They are going to go on to the next task at hand and you are going to be forgotten about. You may as well have not even been there at all.

So, you need to have a tactic ready — at your disposal — when you hear, "Let me think about it."

Say this: "OK. Good. But, so that I can be sure that I've done my job here today and you have everything you need to think about, let me ask you a question: What is holding you back?" Or, "What do you need to think about?" Or, "What's not clear?" Then use the message in Tool #12. Shut up.

If you get nothing in response other than, "I just need to think about it," try this: "OK. Let me try a quick checklist before I leave. Is the price a point of concern?" Silence. If they say, "Yes," you've got yourself a true negative objection and you know what to do about that because we went through that in detail back in Tool #8. If they say, "No," then you check that off as not being something for them to have to think about. "Is the product specification list a match for what you need?" The answer to that will be the same thing. It's either a true negative objection or a misunderstanding objection or it isn't a problem. Either way, you know what to do. If that isn't a problem, then you continue, "Is it that you don't see how what I am offering here is the right match for what you really need?" If they say, "Yes," then you have an indifference objection or perhaps a misunderstanding but you know what to do and it isn't leave. It's go back and handle that objection and then close again.

174]

If you deplete your checklist of everything you can think of that they need to think about — there's nothing left — then you simply and sincerely ask, "Then, what is there left to think about? That's all there is. May we go ahead and get started?" Silence.

The customer has to either give you an objection, give you a "No," or give you a "Yes." The logic of sticking to their stance that they need to think about it is gone. It makes no sense to think about something when there is nothing to think about.

This process is a chance for you to close again after the prospect has had a complete and fair opportunity to "check off" all the things about which they must think. They do their thinking right here and right now. And, why not? Frankly, they're most likely not going to think about it. They're going to put it aside and forget it and do nothing. That's wrong.

This is one of those weird situations where you are hoping for an objection. That's because when you run your checklist and the buyer says, "Yes, I'm concerned about timing" or references or price or whatever, the stall has vanished and been replaced by an objection. You are better off with an objection to handle than you are with a stall and nothing to handle except your anxiety while you wait for the inevitable, "No."

So, this is (rather than "No, But, If," as we will discuss in detail in the next Tool) "OK, but..." When they say, "Let me think about it," you happily say, "<u>OK, but</u>, so that we can be sure you have everything you need to think about, let me ask you some really quick questions. Is it this? Is it that?" Keep asking until you can't think of anything else for them to think about. If they stop you on one item, that's good news because that's an objection to deal with and the stall has vanished. If they don't stop you on any of the items, then there's nothing to think about and you should simply close again.

The Committee Stall

None of that will work for a Committee Stall. That's because, with a Committee Stall, the customer isn't saying that he needs to think about it. He's saying that he must consult with others before giving you an answer. He can't — or won't — make the decision to buy without talking to other people first.

Whoa. That's not his fault. That's our fault. Why didn't we already know this? Were we trying to sell something to someone who does not have the authority to buy it? Did we not qualify this buyer prior to getting to this point. Ouch. That's our fault.

Or, maybe this person is only one decision maker among many. In Tool #6 we discussed Different Customer Roles. If we are talking to an economic decision maker who is going to have to consult with a technical person who will ultimately evaluate the features of our proposal against the needs of their internal processes, certainly we should have already expected that we were going to get a Committee Stall when we attempted to close. If we're surprised now, it's our fault.

We should have asked, long ago, "Is this a decision that you will be making on your own or will you be consulting with others before deciding?" If, long ago, they told us, "This is my decision alone," it is very difficult for them to spring a Committee Stall on us now. If, long ago, they told us "Yes, I will be consulting with others," then we have a whole different ball game and we knew it up front.

If they tell us that they will be consulting with others before deciding, you say this, "OK. Great. Then instead of asking you to say 'Yes' when we're done here, I'll be instead asking you whether or not you are willing to recommend to the others involved that they say 'Yes,' if my proposal satisfies their unmet needs as well as it does yours."

"How's that?" They'll either say "Yes" or "No." If they are reasonable, they need to say "Yes" here.

You then are in a position to say, "Perfect. I'm going to convince you today and then I'll be able to provide you with proof and backup so you'll be able to convince them too."

Again, go back to Tool #6 and do your homework.

Albert Einstein is quoted as having said, "Insanity is doing the same thing over and over again and expecting different results." When a customer stalls, they are committing themselves to not changing; in effect, they are committing themselves to doing the same thing over and over again that they have always been doing. You and I are there because we uncovered an unmet need not being satisfied by what they are currently doing over and over again. That's why I say that stalls are wrong and customers are wrong when they stall. When they stall, they are committing themselves to keep doing the same thing for a while longer. Nothing will change for them. Their unmet need will continue to be unmet. That's not a good thing.

Taking this notion a step further, it's important to think back on personality types. Remember, High S types are highly prone to stalling because of their dislike for change. High C types are highly prone to stalling because of their fear of changing to something worse than what they are currently doing. And, High I types are highly prone to stalling if they fear the change they authorize will irritate or aggravate others.

We owe it to them to fight off these stalls. That's our job.

[177

WHAT I WOULD HAVE DONE DIFFERENTLY
IF I KNEW THEN WHAT I KNOW NOW

I would never have accepted another stall without having fought it and fought it hard. Now, I would never have wanted to burn a bridge by fighting so hard that I got thrown out and told to never return. But, I would have been willing to leave a bridge smoldering; fighting hard to turn this "Maybe later," into either a "Yes" or a "No" now. Even a "No," you ask? Yes. That's because "No" is what stalls inevitably become.

WHAT YOU SHOULD DO RIGHT NOW

Learn and use the tactics for "Let Me Think About It Stalls" and "Committee Stalls."

You'll have less stress in your life waiting for that "No" that will come later and you will probably find that you'll get more "Yes" answers now because you wouldn't take "Let Me Think About It" for an answer. The other person who will have less stress in their life is your boss – the person who is awaiting the "Yes" you implied. Remember, your boss is reassuring his/her boss that this deal is going to close. Do you want your boss and your boss' boss to lose confidence in you? No? Don't accept stalls.

For more on addressing stalls, take a look at our ej4 video, "Defeating Stalls," located at STUNselling.com/stalls.

TOOL #11

No, But, If™

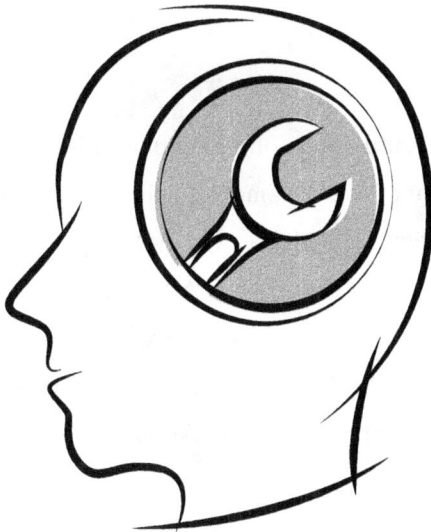

Here's What You're Going to Learn

Once a prospect accepts that he might actually buy what you are selling, if he is good, he will begin to nibble away at you. He will ask for a concession in terms such as a better price or a quicker delivery or a slower payment date. If you allow him to take that first bite, he will nibble again and again until you stop him. Why wouldn't he? It's working. To stop the nibbling, you must nibble back. You do that by never saying "Yes" to a nibble. Instead, even if the nibble is one you are willing to concede, you must say "No. I can't do that. But, I can do this IF you will do that."

No, But, If works wonders.

THE POINT

Stop customer nibbling by nibbling back.

While working for Anita Marx, the executive director of the Anheuser-Busch Beer Marketing Management Institute, something I started in 1987 and that continued until 2004, I met an intriguing fellow by the name of Paul Wineman. Paul, a rare American who speaks Farsi, has experience negotiating in Iran, Saudi Arabia and across the Middle East after he finished a stint in Tehran as the US Army Airborne-Special Forces Advisor to the Imperial Iranian Army. Paul is one interesting guy to say the very least.

While I consulted with and taught Anheuser-Busch and its wholesaler family a variety of selling skills and other things, Paul stuck strictly to negotiations. He has even written a book, *The Sweet Art of Negotiation*, which you can find on Amazon.

Anita asked me to work with Paul to remove some jargon from his repertoire but, instead, I added some.

He taught a process that involved telling a negotiation adversary "No," to just about anything they asked for. He then would circle back around and ask them for something after having arrived at some concession to use as an enticement.

I slept on it and finally came up with the label we use at ej4, "No, But, If". So, whatever I write in this chapter, its genesis comes from and most of the credit (if you like it) goes to Paul.

Simply put, it works like this: You are selling. The prospect has accepted what you are offering in principle but is seeking a sweetener before saying "Yes." The prospect begins to "nibble."

"Can you give me better pricing?" the prospect asks. You, wanting to make the sale, offer up whatever discount you are authorized to give. "OK," the prospect says. "May I have 180 day payment terms?" he nibbles again. "Uh, I can probably swing that," you say. Before you have a chance to close, he says "How about free goods? I was thinking one free with ten," he nibbles once more.

Why would he not continue to nibble? You are saying, "Yes." To be frank, he would be a fool to stop nibbling until you say, "No."

If you are like most sellers I have had the pleasure to work with, you are petrified at the very idea of saying "No," to a prospect. You will go to great lengths to never say, "No," to anything when you are selling. You say, "Sure, Uh-huh, OK," because you think that will get you closer to the ultimate sale. You believe that if you just give in on this one itty bitty request then the prospect will thank you gratefully and reach out his hand and say, "OK, then. Write up my order. You've got a customer." Of course, that has never happened to any of us but, still, we can hope can't we?

Worse, instead of saying "Yes," you say, "Uh, let me ask my boss." That's really a dumb idea. First of all, the prospect hears that as a "Yes, my boss has the authority to do this thing you ask that I do not have the authority to do and I will plead your case until my boss gives in and you get what you want."

Let me talk to my boss.

That's not what you said but it is what the buyer heard. Plus, this nibble functions as a perfect stall because you aren't going to get this deal now until you go to your boss and get approval. You have no hope of getting out of this mess today unless you phone your boss up right now, reach him or her, plead your case, get your concession agreed to and then give the good news to your prospect. But, if your prospect is a tough customer, since that nibble worked, they will now attempt to take another bite out of your hide. Why wouldn't they? The last attempt worked; you didn't say "No." Your boss didn't say, "No." Only a very poor buyer would stop when they were only ahead this far when you are giving all the signals that they can make a better deal with you if they just keep asking for more concessions.

Paul's point — and my point here — is that until you nibble back, your customer is going to take bite after bite after bite out of your hide.

You've got to stop him. But, how? You can't say "No" to a customer, especially a tough customer. They'll throw you out on your ear. "Just say no!" the phrase coined by First Lady Nancy Reagan to an Oakland, CA, elementary school student back in 1982, sounds good but works less well than one might think. There must be something better than just saying "No."

There is something better; much better. Use No, But, If.

The No, But, If Sequence

When the prospect asks, "Can you give me better pricing?" You remorsefully say, "No." To avoid being kicked out of the prospect's office, you quickly reopen the door you just slammed shut by saying, "But, I can achieve the same result by letting you earn a quantity discount if you will order a full truck load." Then, silence.

Note the rhythmic sequencing of what you just said: NO, [185 (I cannot do what you asked) BUT (I can do a different thing that will still get you what you want) IF (you will do something to sweeten the deal for me in return). When you use No, But, If, you stop giving anything up without getting anything in return and you bring a fast halt to the aggravating but ever-present customer behavior of nibbling.

When the prospect asks, "May I have 180 day payment terms?" You say, "No. Payment terms of that length aren't possible. But, I could get you a 2% discount if you paid the full amount in 30 days." Then, silence.

There's your No, But, If sequence again.

When the prospect asks, "How about free goods?" You say, "No. I don't have any free goods to offer. But, I could get you practically the same financial benefit if you would agree to a 200 case front end cap display for the next two weeks at a reduced retail price." Then, silence.

There's the No, But, If sequence once more.

It is critical for me to point out that you must execute this tactic perfectly or it could do you harm.

First, understand that the "No," coming out of your mouth may shock the buyer a bit, particularly if they are a High D or, possibly High C, buyer. They don't expect you to say "No." No other seller has the courage to say "No," to them so it will come as a great surprise that you are different. It might even make them angry.

You, however, move quickly before they have the opportunity to get angry, without delay or hesitation, by saying "But." That "But" word saves you. I just checked the online dictionary for their definition of the word "But" and I found this: "Used to indicate the impossibility of anything other than what is being stated." I have an easier definition for the word. The definition of the word "But" is: "Everything I said before this isn't true."

Think about it. "You are a nice person, but..." The speaker is preparing you for news that you're not a very nice person. "We have plenty of time to get there on time but..." The speaker is preparing you for the news that we're going to be late. "You look great in that outfit but..." The speaker is getting ready to tell you that you don't look great in that outfit.

When using the No, But, If tactic, what you are saying, then, is this: "I just said 'No' BUT I'm getting ready to turn that 'No' into a 'Yes.'

In other words, keep listening because the 'No' won't count when you hear the rest of what I have to say."

"No, I can't do that. But, I can do this other thing which will benefit you just as much or nearly as much, if you will do something nice for me in return." No, But, If puts you in the position of nibbling back. That will usually stop the nibbling process emanating from them but who cares? If you always get something in return whenever you are forced to give something up, then both you and the prospect are getting something good. It's a win/win approach to sales — in fact, to life.

How to Use No, But, If...

- "No, I can't do that. Wish I could; just can't. But, here is a different thing that I am able to do to offer you up an extra benefit. However, you will have to give me something in return."... or... [187

- "No, I can't do that. Wish I could; just can't. But, in lieu of what you are asking for, I can do this other thing which, while not the same and while maybe not as good for you is, nonetheless, pretty good for you."

You have just psychologically clobbered the buyer and almost instantly picked them right back up again. You're not finished, however. Get something for yourself in return. "No, I can't do that. Wish I could; just can't. But, I can do this other thing if you will do this thing over here for me." You have just psychologically offered the buyer something which they must earn by giving you something back in return.

The expression "tit for tat" (this for that) was, according to multiple dictionary definitions, first coined in the 1500s. Dictionary.com expands by saying, "An equivalent given in return or retaliation; blow for blow." Wikipedia gets the expression all the way to "Quid Pro Quo," from the Latin, "Something for something." Either way, that's the point, isn't it?

"Mr. Customer, I'll give you something if you give me something in return. I'll give you something if you give an equivalent something in return." Seems fair, doesn't it? It not only seems fair; it is fair. And, it generally puts a stop to them asking for something for nothing. That's what you and I want: To stop giving up something for nothing in order to make the sale.

The point is that you're going to do something for them, but you'll do that something only if you get something back, something in return. Never give anything away for nothing. Always get something back.

Watch Out!

There are a few things to watch out for when using "No, But, If."

First, when you say, "No," sound sad to be saying it. You cannot be overly aggressive when saying "No" in such a way that your prospect hears you as being arrogant or immovable or unreasonable. You need to sound remorseful; almost as if you really wish you could — you really do — but, sadly, you just can't; it's not within your power to do so. It's not possible and you are sad about that. Certainly you can't sound like a parent disciplining a child with that long and cautionary, "Noooo," that we've all said to our kids. This is a buyer, not someone over whom we have complete control like our young offspring. You've got to assume the correct voice tone. There is no way that I can figure out to let you hear the perfect way to say, "No," on this printed page. But, when you watch the ej4 video that accompanies this chapter, you will see some examples of the perfect voice tone and inflection to use when saying, "No."

You can accompany your "No" with a visible droop in posture that says you're not happy to be saying no. You just have no choice and you're feeling a bit defeated when you say it. "Man, I'm sorry to have to say 'No' to you on this, but I have no choice."

Another tactic that will make "No, But, If" work even better is to know in advance what you want in return so that you are ready to ask for it without having to think about it. And, make sure you can express what you want in return in as few words as possible. This tactic works best when it is succinct and concise.

One more thing: After you tell your prospect what you want in return in as few words as possible, shut up. You will read much more about this "shut up" advice in the next Tool. Much more.

[189

You should expect the process of using silence after your completed "No, But, If" retort to be very difficult at first. But, if you let the customer off the hook by talking during the critical few moments when the customer is weighing getting what you're asking for in return for getting what he is asking for you destroy his train of thought and evaluation process. Be silent. Wait. Watch the customer's eyes for what is happening behind them in the brain. The brain is a powerful thing but you've got to give it a few moments to do its thing. Thinking takes time.

Be ready. It is tough when you're on the spot to quickly figure out everything you would love for this customer to do for you when, in fact, your brain is focused on what you are offering to do for him. I suggest making a list of everything you could get from "the perfect customer" to make your ultimate deal truly "win/win." Think this up; make a list. Do it in advance. Be ready for your "If" statements.

It makes sense to also think in advance about what concessions you are willing to make when you say "But." I often think that too many sellers start out with their best possible price and their best possible terms and their best possible quality of product in advance and leave themselves nothing to offer when the prospect wants better than their best.

And...

One final tip is this: If, when you are silent after you deliver your masterful "No, But, If" message, they are also silent and, after much time has passed and you just can't stand it anymore because your palms are sweating and your heart is beating out of your chest, try tossing out a close. Say, "What do you say?" or "Do we have a deal?" Then what? You guessed it. More silence. In any event, understand that to break the silence after a "No, But, If" message ruins what you are trying to do. Break it only with a close.

Don't be a pushover. Don't be easy. Be tough. When you are asked for something, always ask for something in return.

A Quick Story...

While at dinner with a high-ranking retail executive, that person's mobile phone rang. The call was coming from a manager at one of their stores. A big ticket item was about to be sold, but the potential purchaser was asking for a big discount — a discount that was beyond the calling manager's ability to grant. My dinner companion had the authority, but also bore the ultimate responsibility for margin and profitability. Unlike the manager, my companion wanted to make a profit on the sale rather than just make the sale.

My dinner companion used the No, But, If tactic twice.

First, to the manager, these words were said: "No. I won't authorize a discount that deep because we'll lose money on the sale. But, I will authorize a discount that is half that size if your customer will also buy the product protection insurance from us which they should do anyway on an item this valuable." [191

Then, a second use of the tactic was delivered to the caller. "Tell them, 'No. We can't go that deep or we'll lose money. But, we can go half as much if you'll buy the product protection plan.' Tell them that and see what they say. Good Luck."

My companion used "No, But, If" on the manager and then gave the manager the "No, But, If" script to use on the manager's customer.

Later, we learned that the purchase took place and everybody was happy. No, But, If kept the retailer from losing the sale and also from losing the profit on the sale. The discount on the goods was offset by the profit from the product protection plan. The customer had an insurance policy should the big ticket item be lost or stolen. It was a win/win.

The rest of the meal was, for me, much more tasty because our little No, But, If tactic worked. It usually does.

WHAT I WOULD HAVE DONE DIFFERENTLY
IF I KNEW THEN WHAT I KNOW NOW

I would have never never never given anything away as a concession without at least trying to get something of equal or greater value to me back in return.

When the high school principal asked for a discount on the publishing contract price, I would have said, "No. I can't discount the price on a one year deal. But, I can guarantee you an equal savings on this year's and next year's books if you will sign a multi-year contract with me." Then silence.

When the corporate training director asked me for a discount on my per diem fee for an in-person training seminar, I would have said, "No. I can't discount my daily rate. But, I can give you extra value by providing a follow up skill reminder letter to each participant if you'll agree to the price I have proposed." In that way, the training director would not have saved any money, but would have received better retention of the skills that we trained during the seminar through a positive pressure reminder.

WHAT YOU SHOULD DO RIGHT NOW

First, think of all the things, other than list price, that would benefit you when you make a sale. Payment up front, extra-charge warranties, deeper stocking of more SKUs (Stock Keeping Units—or Items—for those of you who don't use this term), display support or advertising support, better position in the resale proposition — either in the store or on the web site, or, well, whatever would benefit you.

[193

Second, think of all the things, other than price, that would benefit them when you make the sale that you could offer without breaking your bank.

You need to be quick on your feet. So, prior knowledge of knowing what to say after "But" (here's what I can do for you) and knowing what to say after "If" (here's what you can do for me) is critical. As I learned when I was an Eagle Scout, "Be Prepared."

Take a look at the ej4 video, "No, But, If," located at STUNselling.com/nobutif for a better understanding of this concept.

TOOL # 12

When to Shut Up

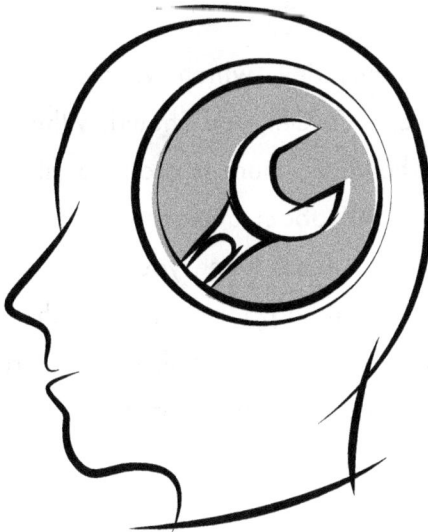

Here's What You're Going to Learn

Selling is not about talking.

Selling is not about presenting.

Selling is about engaging in a conversation.

It's a dialog rather than a monologue. Talking and presenting can only stop when you are willing to engage in silence. But, how do you know when to shut up? Read on.

THE POINT

Customers are not engaged unless they are talking. For them to talk, you have to shut up.

At first glance, the QuickSell, which we discussed in Tool #3, is comprised of four steps: To Get, You Should, Which Would, I Could. If you read closely, however, there is a critical fifth step: Shut Up. If you closely read Tool #8 about overcoming objections, again, you read the advice to "Shut Up." Once you have delivered your short answer for a misunderstanding, for example, "Shut Up." In Tool #1, Determining Customer Needs, we talked about asking questions. Once a question is posed, the questioner has to "Shut Up" so the customer can answer.

I'm sorry to use such impolite language as "Shut Up." I could be much more civilized and say "Hush," "Be Silent," "Do Not Speak," or some other more polite phrase. The problem is that, for me at least, "Shut Up" is somehow the perfect way to express what I am recommending.

Being quiet — knowing when to not talk — is a critical skill that is, from my experience, extremely lacking in most sales people.

Any exceptions? Sure. Being silent is an offense worthy of termination if you are a radio personality. In the summer of 1969 while a student at what was then known as Kansas State College of Pittsburg, I found a job working as an announcer/director at KOAM-TV. The job was pretty simple. I was to be in the audio booth to deliver station identification tags at the appropriate times. "You're watching KOAM-

TV, Channel 7, Pittsburg, Kansas; NBC Color for Mid-America." If the seven second time slot for those words was filled with silence, I would be fired. In the broadcasting business, silence is known as "dead air."

Dead air in the selling business is one of many keys to success. When a question is posed, it should be followed by silence; dead air. When a close is attempted, it should be followed by silence; dead air. Whenever a seller wants a buyer to talk, the easiest way to make that happen is through seller's silence, dead air. So when you ask a question, when you try to close or when you just want your prospect to talk, zip it!

Our job as sellers is to find the prospect's unmet need and then STUN by using the QuickSell, by saying, "To get (your unmet need fulfilled), you should (buy from me) which would (deliver the benefit that clearly meets the unmet need). I could (tell what you will do in the form of a close — a question)." After you deliver that, you've got to shut up. Don't keep talking. Be quiet. Zip it. Create dead air.

When you do that, you "put the ball in the prospect's court" so to speak.

In my leader-led sales training seminar days, I always carried a tennis ball. I would demonstrate the power of silence by choosing a participant to do a mini-role-play with me. Whoever was holding the ball was the only person allowed to speak; the other person had to wait silently until given the ball. In one common scenario, I would ask an open question and, on the last word of the question, toss the tennis ball to my prospect-playing partner. Then, I would stand silently. My role play partner would answer and, at the end of their reply, toss the ball back to me. I would say, let's do it again and the next time I would ask the same open question and, on the last word of the question, I would ramble on, never tossing the ball. In effect, I never put the ball into the prospect's "court." The illustration worked beautifully. The prospect never had the pressure to speak or reply. All the pressure stayed with me just as the tennis ball did. As a seller, that is counter-intuitive.

Most sellers think the pressure is on them when they quit talking but in reality the pressure, when the seller falls silent, falls to the prospect who, psychologically, feels the need to fill the dead air. The only way the prospect can do that is by speaking — answering the question or responding to the validity of the benefit match to their unmet need.

> Silence is golden in that it results in a sale;
> the seller gets the gold.

It is hard to stay silent when the prospect also remains quiet. But, think about it. If you asked a question the prospect is pondering a reply. Don't let them off the hook by breaking the silence. Let them think about it. Be silent. If your question was a closing question such as, "Do we have a deal?" then continuing to speak allows the prospect to exist without pressure. The ball never goes into his or her court.

I've heard it countless times.

Seller, "You need this, we've got that which gives you what you need. Can I write up an order?" Then the seller stands mute. But, after a couple of seconds of silence on the part of the buyer, the seller panics and begins to speak again. "I mean, you can see that this is a good idea. You will benefit greatly." An observer can feel the tension in the room as the seller babbles on. The buyer thinks, "Why is this person so unsure of himself? Why doesn't he give me a chance to think for a second and say, 'Yes'? Maybe this isn't such a good deal."

The only thing that can occur when the seller goes silent after asking a question is that the prospect replies. The reply could conceivably be a "Yes." In that case, the deal is done or, at least, the question is answered in the affirmative. The reply could be a "No." In that case, a quick follow up of "Why no?" offers the seller the opportunity to hear and understand the buyer's reason or objection. That reason or objection is just another unmet need. The seller has a new shot at a fresh QuickSell.

Using "The Circle" which we cited earlier, you can again see the value of silence.

> "Mrs. Customer, you need this. <u>Is that correct</u>?"
> Silence so the prospect has the opportunity to say, "Yes."
> (i.e., to nod)
>
> "Well, I have this for you," the seller says, "which will do this (discuss the benefit of what is being offered)."
>
> "<u>That's what you want, isn't it</u>?" Now, more silence so the prospect again has the opportunity to say, "Yes." (i.e., to nod)
>
> Then, the seller closes. "May I have your signature on this order?" Silence.
>
> These two underlined questions are known as "nod questions." They are designed to get the customer to give you a nod which is a buying sign.

> If you have the need right and you ask correctly, this is powerful. "You told me about what was happening to you and, from that, it seems to me that you need a more reliable delivery of raw materials. <u>Am I hearing you correctly</u>?"
>
> "Yes," said while nodding slightly.
>
> "I can reserve product from our warehouse for you immediately and deliver it on the exact timetable you specify. That timely delivery means no more interruptions in your manufacturing process. <u>That's what you need, right</u>?"
>
> "Yes, that's what we need," the prospect says while again nodding.
>
> The last question continues the "nod momentum" stimulus begun by the first question and serves as a set up for a close. As the seller prompts the buyer to nod not once but twice before the close, it is more likely than not that the buyer will again say "Yes," in effect continuing the momentum set up by the first two nod questions.

Me: *"As a seller, you need to close more effectively. Is that accurate?"* Silence.

You: *"Yes."* (Said with a nod of your head.)

Nod!
Nod!
Nod!

Me: *"If you use the psychological circle of selling, you clearly show what the customer needs and that what you are offering meets that need. That means he is more likely to say, 'Yes.' That's what you want, isn't it?"* Silence.

You: *"Sure."* (Again, said while nodding.)

Me: *"OK, then. Can I sign you up?"* Silence.

You will feel a momentum that keeps your head nodding. When your head is nodding up and down, it is impossible to say, "No."

This is a powerful tool. It is almost as if you had some super glue and a piece of string. You glue the string to the prospect's chin and you can force him to nod whenever you tug the string. Nod questions are like super glue and a string. They work. "You want nods, right?" I'm tugging; are you nodding?

If you talk through a nod, it negates the power of the moment and momentum does not occur. Be silent after you ask that nod question and give the prospect the opportunity to begin nodding. It will get you to your successful close in a beautiful way.

I believe in an economy of words and a lot of silence. I urge you to try it.

You know from Tool #5 regarding DISC, our customers have different personalities. They respond to silence in different ways.

If you keep talking to a High D, he thinks you're trying to manipulate him or take advantage of him. You've got to let him talk. That way, he gets to radiate power and prestige as his natural aura. You, by listening to him — never interrupting — become, in his mind, submissive. He is dominant; he needs someone to dominate. That's you. But, only if you are silent. When he finishes his speech, either answer whatever objection he's raised followed by a "That's what you need, isn't it?" or, if he has not given you an objection ask, "So, it makes sense for us to move forward with an order, do you agree?" Silence. Shut up. The ball is in his court and that's where he likes it. He's not a great listener anyway. The less you talk, the less he has to listen. When you're quiet, he sees that as a sign of respect — something he demands. Don't smile and nod too much with a High D. That makes you appear to be more in control and, in the mind of a High D, that's a bad thing. The D is in control at all times and you need to show that you understand that. Be serious as you shut up.

If you keep talking to a High I, he doesn't get to talk. High I's love to talk, they love to smile and expound on whatever is important to them. They need a good listener. That's you. But, always remember, you can only be listening when you are silent. You can nod and smile and, if you absolutely must, mutter an "uh huh," or "you're right." Mostly, though, shut up. If you keep talking, he can't talk. He can't tell you what he knows. He can't tell you, even more importantly, what he feels. He needs to talk; you need to be silent and listen. Smile and nod when the High I talks. That makes you appear to be in agreement and receptive to what is being said and that's a good thing. The I wants you to like him and smiles and nods broadcast that. Be happy as you shut up. The voice of a High I is sweet music to the High I. Let them sing as you listen approvingly and, I hope this word isn't overdoing it, lovingly.

If you keep talking to a High S, you are robbing him of the chance to "think out loud." This person likes things as they are; you represent a change from that, an alteration of the safe status quo. As they respond to your benefit statements, they are weighing pros and cons aloud, working through the details of change that cause them fear or simply reacting aloud to what you've been saying as they evaluate the risks involved of what you've been saying. Stay silent. Let them work it through. They're just as likely to give in and accept your proposition as they are to object to it. Give them a minute. Be silent.

If you talk too much, you seem like a "smooth talking devil," the one's they've heard about. They buy because of trust. They never trust sellers who talk too much and don't show respect through silence and the process of listening to their fears and concerns. If you rattle on, you succeed only in rattling him. That's not a winning plan with a High S.

The High C is concerned with perfection and risk avoidance. He needs time to think about what you are proposing and the opportunity to think through the ramifications of what you are proposing. If you keep talking, you interrupt the High C's evaluation process. The C strives for perfection and that means that he must be certain that what you are proposing is the best thing for him. He cannot and will not evaluate quickly. Through silence, you give him precious time to cross the T's and dot the i's.

[203

None of this should be taken to mean that you don't push. What you do is push and then shut up.

When the customer ultimately says, "Yes," thank them and get out of there. If you break the silence with more benefits or a recap of how your product meets their needs you may talk yourself out of the sale. Again, silence works in your favor, but this time the silence is accompanied by your absence. Get out of there.

Silence is golden. Remember that.

WHAT I WOULD HAVE DONE DIFFERENTLY
IF I KNEW THEN WHAT I KNOW NOW

I would have been much less fearful of failure because I would have been much less fearful of dead air. Fear is a bad thing in a seller. Buyers sense it. Silence communicates confidence. Confidence (not arrogance) is a good thing. Simply put, I would have known when to shut up. I would have known that the time to shut up is after a question is posed and after a close is attempted.

204]

WHAT YOU SHOULD DO RIGHT NOW

Practice silence. With a friend or your spouse or significant other, try a bit of silence. Let them talk while you silently listen. If that person is a High D or High C, nod subtly and respectfully. If they are a High I, smile and nod vigorously. If they are a High S, nod respectfully and patiently. You'll see it work. They will be impressed with your willingness to listen. People love people who listen to them. And, what more can you want from a spouse or significant other than their love?

[205

Can you get your customers to love you? Try a bit of silence and see if it helps them to raise you up on a pedestal not occupied by the other people who call on them. That's a great place to sit.

Want a few reminders of why silence is so golden? Watch the ej4 video, "When to Shut Up," located at STUNselling.com/shut_up.

TOOL # 13

Selling in New Products

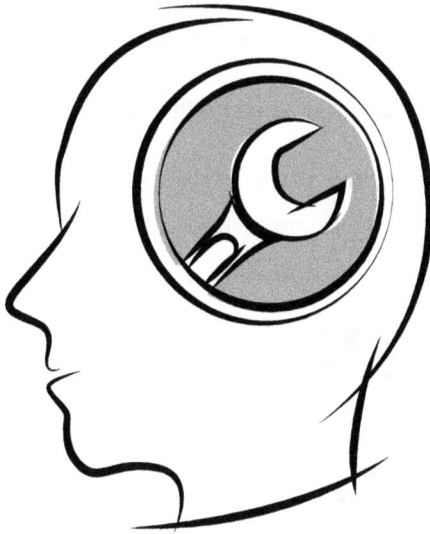

Here's What You're Going to Learn

You already have a relationship with a customer
and suddenly the marketing people announce
that there is a new product for you to sell.

The way you get that second or twenty-second product or service
into the customer isn't the same as how you sold in the first one.

THE POINT

It might seem as though it would be easier to sell in a new product to an existing customer, but reality is often just the opposite.

"Oh, no. Not another new product. Now what?"

That could be your voice. Or, it could be the voice of your current customer.

Let's start with you. A new product means new features and benefits to learn along with new pricing, where and how marketing thinks this should be positioned (and hopefully what unmet customer need it is

designed to satisfy), what the sales margin and volume goals are for its launch, whether or not it can be produced in the needed quantity, whether it can be delivered as promised, whether or not it will actually work, whether or not it will cannibalize the existing line; oh, my.

You may have an attitude about it. You may be excited about it. Whatever you feel about it, IT is here. Will you have time to give it adequate attention? Does this mean that you must call on every one of your existing accounts overnight to roll it out? Does this mean that you must call on all the accounts assigned to you, but where you have no current business and start over with them? If so, is that good news for you because it is a reason to go back and light a fire? Or, is it bad news because they told you to get lost and never come back, but now your manager says you've got to go back and try again with these people who are clearly jerks? Harrumph!

Now, how about your existing customers' point of view? Assuming they also buy products from people other than you, they see one heck of a lot more new products than you do. Most of those new products will be things to which they will have to say, "No." Saying "No," is unpleasant for both parties. New products mean new specifications to get to users to validate adequacy. Do these new products mean that all those jerks you told to get lost and never come back are about to come back because now their managers are saying they've got to come back and try again and, by the way, they are clearly jerks? Do you have the space for this? What will our company have to drop to allow for this new product to be introduced? Will it cannibalize what we're already doing so there is no incremental gain? Will it cost more and wreak havoc with our budgets? Harrumph!

[209

Yes; new products are a true good news/bad news occurrence.

New products are a fact of life for everyone who intends to be in business a year or two from now. If you're standing still, you're losing ground. Yesterday's reality is old news today… time to move forward in order to survive. The really bad news happens when a competitor comes out with something new and, oh my gosh, it's really good. We're in trouble. Where is our product development team on this; are they asleep at the wheel? I'll bet Kodak and Royal Typewriter and Oldsmobile and TiVo and Bowmar (look them up) and a whole bunch of other people who worked at those places wished that somebody had the brains to come up with something new a long, long time ago.

When it comes to new products, there are two things that customers usually fight over; if you know what they are, you are more likely to win the fight. Your customer has two things on his mind all the time:

1. **Number of accounts**. In retail, they call it store traffic. In finance it may be called the book of business. The pool guy probably calls it pools. Unless you sell to consumers, whoever you sell to have people that they sell to as well. Will your new product help them get some new customers? If your new product will help your customers to gain new customers, you're going to help them to make money.

2. **Amount of volume and profit each existing customer currently generates**. In retail is may be called average transaction size or average check. In finance, maybe it's dollars on deposit or under management. The pool guy probably calls it chemicals to pool owners. Will your new product help them get their customers to spend more with them? If your new product will help your customers to get their current customers to spend more, you're going to help their companies to make money.

So here's the thing: If your customer doesn't really want to deal with a new product then that's not unusual. What would be truly unusual would be if your customer didn't want the new "traffic" your product will draw or the higher "check" he achieves from his customers.

[211

If you think about new products in these terms, then you really aren't selling new products at all. Instead you are selling things that drive one or both of your customers' revenue streams. It is a good bet that even if they don't really want your new product, they do really want what your new product is going to do for them.

A problem arises when your new product needs a bit of help to achieve gains for your customer. Promotion, advertising, point of sale material and training are all potential examples of the help that may be required. In most businesses, that help is your responsibility. Hopefully, your marketing department is on top of this. If not, you'll have to be.

If ever there was a place for the QuickSell, this is it; see Tool #3. You'll have to have figured out the unmet need for this new product; see Tool #1. You'll need to have learned the feature/benefit relationships; see Tool #4. There may be new users or approvers scattered across the customer enterprise that you'll have to sell; see Tool #6. Are you dealing with High S buyers? High D buyers? You need a different approach with these two because what you are bringing to them is a change; see Tool #5. When you've got those figured out, you're off to a great start.

If ever there was a place to be prepared for objections, this is it; see Tool #8. There will be misunderstandings so you need your short straight answers to be ready to go. There will be doubts. You'll need proof sources for those. Check with marketing and product development. There will be indifference. That one is yours. Why do they need it? See Tool #1 again. And, there will be true negatives in the new product because nothing is perfect. That means you need to do your homework to compare accurately your entry to the competitions' existing offerings.

The point here is that a successful new product rollout is a grand undertaking that is fraught with peril and requires precise execution to earn an acceptable return on investment for the capital that went into research and development to get us to this point.

There is a lot riding on this; there is a lot riding on you.

My consumer product company clients were always coming out with new products. Years ago, Pepsi, without a viable lemon lime soft drink, came out with Slice. But it wasn't just Lemon Lime Slice. It was Orange Slice, Grape Slice and even Apple Slice. It was not a lemon lime. It was a complete flavor lineup. Retailors asked the Pepsi sales rep if he or she had shelf-stretchers because there was no room for one new item let alone a whole set of new products. The marketing and product development people in Purchase, New York, where Pepsi was headquartered, didn't really bother themselves with that. It was up to the sales people, both front line and key account representatives, to figure out how to meet the goals that were set. The problem was that without marketing and product development understanding, the reality of the customers' shelf and cooler space, the Slice brand lineup was off to a shaky start. The proof? Do you see a lot of Apple or Grape Slice in your neighborhood store? I thought not.

Then, there is the customer who feels as though you've already got enough business with them. Are you greedy or what? Will you only be satisfied when you sell everything to them and your competition sells nothing to them? Who do you think you are?

Do you have time? One would assume that you're not knocking off early every day because you don't have enough to sell.

Here's the point of this chapter: When you get a new product, you're obligated to go back to the drawing board and start afresh. There are lots of things to put in place ranging from how you manage your territory to how well you can re-analyze customer needs to put a STUN in place to discovering that there are new people at the customer organization that you're going to have to meet, figure out and sell to. Yes, there is a lot to take into consideration. If you continue to think about how to satisfy their unmet needs, you are more likely to find success in this very difficult situation.

[213

WHAT I WOULD HAVE DONE DIFFERENTLY
IF I KNEW THEN WHAT I KNOW NOW

I would have been much better prepared. A new product rollout was fraught with peril and expectations were high. My employer had a lot riding on it. I needed to have my "A" game ready and that was not always the case. With my homework half done, I was a poor performer.

WHAT YOU SHOULD DO RIGHT NOW

Get serious about a plan for this new product. The best advice I have is to go Tool by Tool and cover all your bases. In fact, right now, take a look at our ej4 video, "Selling in New Products," located at STUNselling.com/new_products to study up on this topic.

TOOL # 14

Smile

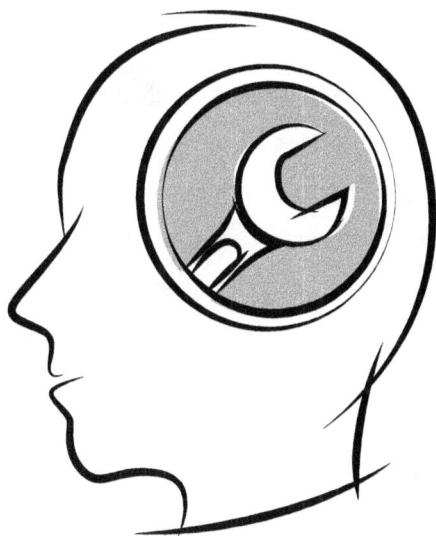

Here's What You're Going to Learn

People like to buy from people they like.

People like people who smile.

THE POINT

Regardless of your personality, you need to smile at people even if it hurts. Please, note, however that the size of your smile depends not on your mood but upon the personality of whoever is viewing it.

I love to walk. My goal is eight miles each day and most days I reach or surpass that. I live in Kansas City, Missouri, and my favorite place to walk there is along the Harry Wiggins Trolley Trail, an abandoned streetcar right of way. I am one of several "regulars" who tend to walk or jog the same parts of the trail at the same times of day. I know not one name of my fellow exercise enthusiasts but I have a warm spot in my heart for those few who smile back at me each morning. On trails such as this one there are those, like me, who smile and gesture at everyone who passes. There are others who avoid eye contact or keep a stern demeanor and they predominate. I'll bet both types are fine human beings but, if given the chance, I would choose to associate with those who smile at me.

On a recent Southwest Airlines flight, my drink order was taken by a flight attendant who smiled as much with her eyes as with her mouth. I think the warmth, if not the sincerity, of a smile is enhanced through eyes. And since we are known for "making eye contact," our smiles are perceived from two different transmission points.

So it goes with most people. The smile is a universal symbol of perceived self-confidence, according to an oft-cited Australasian study authored by Gemma L. Gladstone and Gordon B. Parker who conclude that "Smiling also had a favourable influence upon observer judgements, with subjects who smiled being judged as more likeable and approachable than non-smilers and non-authentic smilers."

Gladstone and Parker close with the idea that while smiles vary, the "very act of smiling might even serve as a self-fulfilling prophecy." And, human smiles are recognized from great distances—one estimate I read says smiles are discernable from 100 yards away. From my time on the Trolley Trail, I am unable to confirm that finding but I can tell whether or not an approaching person is smiling from quite a way off (my vision isn't as sharp at this point in my life as it once was).

All of that is good enough for me. I'm going to smile more. I find it makes me feel good to smile.

But there is more: An article from *Alternative Therapies in Health and Medicine*, a peer reviewed journal, reports that laughter (strongly associated with smiling) "may reduce stress and increase natural killer cell levels, a type of white blood cell that attacks cancer cells."

Finally, in *this* book, the noted author, Paul Russell, writes: "From my experience, smiles help to close sales." Ta Da! (Hope that brought a grin to your face!) I find that I cannot react negatively to an admittedly negative situation when I am smiling. And, I am told by reliable sources (Google it yourself) that the theory of Facial Feedback Hypothesis indicates that how your face appears can affect how you feel about something. In my experience, how you feel about your ability to close a sale is of paramount importance. When you smile, you are telling your brain (or is your brain — in reaction to your smile — telling you?), "I can do this!"

When the going gets tough, the tough get smiling.

Now, how about for the prospect on the other side of the transaction? Smiles are contagious. If you smile, most other human beings will smile back. If they don't, keep smiling. They will begin to wonder if there is something wrong with them, not you.

Smiling makes you more likeable. People like people who smile. And, people like to buy from people they like.

That is not to say that a sale can be made as a result of a smile alone. Years ago, relationship selling was king. Today, people are more pragmatic, more focused on benefits and costs and margins and proof sources. However, when the balance between one vendor and another is pretty even, the sale will always—always—go to the vendor the buyer likes. Your smile, then, is the perfect tiebreaker. And, it is important to realize, it is free. Discounts and payment terms and free goods are all expensive ways to break a tie. Smiles are inexpensive, inexhaustible and infectious.

Another bonus that comes from smiling was uncovered by a 2008 Duke University study entitled, "Orbitofrontal and hippocampal contributions to memory for face-name associations: The rewarding power of a smile." The key finding is that "results demonstrate how rewarding social signals from a smiling face can enhance relational memory for face-name associations." People also like to buy from people whose names they can recall.

Other studies indicate that smiling can enhance your ability to uncover the unmet needs of a prospect, both early in the process and later on when an indifference objection arises. When a speaker is talking to someone who is smiling, they are more likely to offer opinions; but, when they are talking to someone who is frowning, they play it safe by offering up less information. This benefits sellers later in the process as well. If you are attempting to clear up a misunderstanding objection, for example, your straight answer followed by silence is more likely to be accepted. Your proof offered in response to a doubt objection is more likely to be accepted. And, in the case of a true negative objection where you are balancing your shortcoming against your competitor's actual advantage, a smile increases receptivity of the prospect as they balance your benefit list against your shortcoming.

And, silence, when accompanied by a smile, broadcasts confidence. It says to the prospect, "I know you're going to say 'Yes' after you process what I have just told you and I am happy to confidently wait while you do so."

[221]

There are nuances to be thought through as smiling relates to DISC. For example, if you are a High C seller, you may have to work harder at smiling. If you are a High I seller, you have been nodding your head throughout this entire chapter and you're telling yourself, "I already know all of this; you bet, it works!" If you are a High D seller, you are wondering how you can force a smile when you are selling to a buyer that you deem to be unworthy of their position, a dilemma that you find happens to you frequently. (The answer is, to make the sale, you can wear any mask you need to wear comfortable in the knowledge that once you leave this fool's office you can pound your fist onto the elevator door and, even better, yell aloud when you have reached the safety of your car. That mask is your smile.) Finally, if you are a High S seller, you need to get beyond the fear that your smile, particularly if forced, is insincere. But remember, if you are focused on the prospect's needs and your feature really delivers a benefit that satisfies that unmet need, your smile isn't insincere at all because it accompanies the right thing for the prospect to embrace to make their business or their life better.

On the other side of the table sits the prospect. High I buyers will return your smile. The bigger yours is, the bigger theirs becomes. High D buyers will respond favorably to a confident and assertive smile but may recoil from a grin that makes you seem manipulative. Don't try to "out-confident" a High D. Make your smile communicate confidence, not arrogance. High S buyers also react better to a moderate smile. Remember that they need to trust you. Make your smile one that radiates trustworthiness rather than manipulation. And, finally, with High C buyers, smile in a very controlled manner. Ratchet your smile back several notches. These folks, please remember, are logical and not emotional. Every time you make a measured and logical statement that matches your product benefits to their unmet need, you should feel free to accompany it with a "confident semi-grin" that never approaches the level of becoming a smirk.

If your sales call comes right after lunch, make sure you have no bits of kale salad in the crevices of your pearly whites. Mouth debris is distracting and smiles put those unwelcome tidbits on display.

You will help yourself in the process of smiling if you enter into the selling process thinking about how good you are going to feel when you successfully close this deal. If you are a pessimist and fear that your call is going to result in failure then smiling is going to be very difficult. Before you enter onto the field where your sales game is to be played, close your eyes and visualize yourself winning. That visualization of a positive outcome will allow your face to react as it later surely will: with a smile. Another benefit of this tactic is that it extends upward to your eyes. When you successfully close, the smile that comes with that is framed by eyes that, well, twinkle with happiness. Eyebrows dip ever so slightly and your crows' feet crease a bit and a sort of electricity radiates from your baby blues — or browns or greens. Go check yourself out in the mirror. It's all good.

Bobby McFerrin's classic song, "Don't Worry; Be Happy," says it all in a most memorable and most hummable way. "…You might want to sing it note for note."

My favorite part of the song — which had over 36,000,000 YouTube views when I recently watched it, says, "When you're worried your face will frown; that will bring everybody down. So don't worry; be happy." And, of course, when you're happy, you're smiling.

In 1929, Louis Armstrong first recorded these famous words (written by Joe Goodwin, Larry Shay and Mark Fischer and earlier recorded by Duke Ellington): "when you smiling, when you smiling, the whole world smiles with you…" For me, the song should be sung in a slightly different way.

"When you're smiling, when you're smiling, the whole world buys from you."

WHAT I WOULD HAVE DONE DIFFERENTLY
IF I KNEW THEN WHAT I KNOW NOW

This one is easy; I would have smiled even more than I normally did. I would have gotten that crooked tooth I once had fixed much earlier than I did. It never occurred to me how much better my smile would be received until Linda Lee, the wife of my dentist, Hal Lee, suggested that I get a bit of work done. I thought she was being, on my behalf, vain. I thought that spending money on something so frivolous was unworthy of me. But, Linda was right. Hal did a great job. My teeth are straight and my smile is 100 percent; no 1,000 percent better now. And, with a better smile, I would have smiled more and that would have been to my everlasting benefit. If you've got a crooked smile, go see your Linda and Hal and see what it would cost you to have the pearly whites that you'd be more proud to display. The ROI on that may be pretty good.

When I was nervous sitting across the desk from those high school principals in Milwaukee and other far reaches of Wisconsin back in 1974, I would have psyched myself up to smile more. When I was selling sales training services for my first company, the Russell Training Group, Inc., and later for my current and most rewarding enterprise, ej4, I would have smiled more.

THEN... CONTINUED

Now, please understand that this smiling thing gets harder and harder for me as I get older and buyers seemingly get younger. With some of my clients, for example, I have more years of experience dealing with the objections that their salespeople hear from customers than most of their corporate training people could ever imagine. I believe these trainers don't really understand, most of them at least, just what happens in the aisle of that retail store, Walmart, restaurant or office. That may or may not be true.

[225

Fresh approaches and new ideas are critical to the advancement of the enterprise.

However, the selling scripts I read and training videos I see are sometimes far from what the real world presents to us. No experienced seller will adopt an approach advocated in a training tool that doesn't match their real-world experience. So it is critical when a new idea or approach is presented it addresses a real situation and not one that is simply imagined. Everything about the scenario must be perceived as credible or the new idea will be rejected and never attempted — even if it is the best new idea ever.

THEN... CONTINUED

As the "old dog" who, perhaps, is unable to learn a new trick, it is up to me to smile and open my mind to the new idea. Maybe this new idea is better than my old idea. With the smile on my face, I am more open than I would ever be with a frown there instead.

It is to buyers with an attitude or an arrogance or a lack of expertise that I find it most difficult to offer a smile. But, you know what? I am strong. I can wear the mask. And, when I have successfully closed them, I can leave their office and wear the biggest most sincere grin you can imagine because I will have won. I like to win. It makes me happy. And that makes me smile.

WHAT YOU SHOULD DO RIGHT NOW

Go to the mirror. Smile. Look at what a difference it makes in your entire face — not just your mouth. You might even try to laugh at yourself a bit while you smile. Try three different smiles: Low, Medium and High. Look at how your eyes light up!

[227

Now picture yourself on the other side of the table or counter and, from the buyer's perspective, ask yourself, "Would I buy from this person?" Now, get serious. Look in the mirror. How about that person? Who would you rather sit with, talk to, listen to, reveal your secrets to and, ultimately, buy from?

That ought to do it.

Want to practice smiling a bit more? Watch the ej4 video, "Smile!," located at STUNselling.com/smile.

TOOL # 15

Customer Service Later

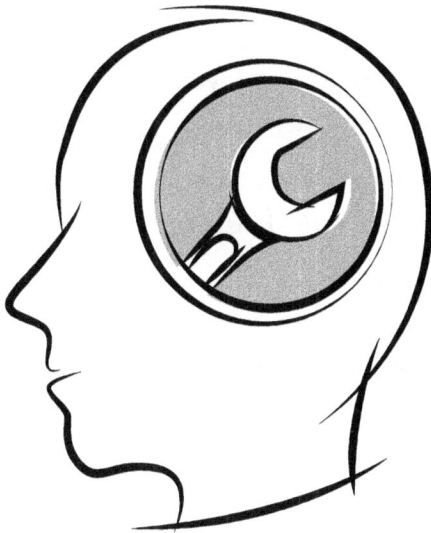

Here's What You're Going to Learn

To grow, you cannot rely solely on new business.

You must maintain what you have in order to gain overall. The way you maintain your current customers is to service their unmet needs with a vigor that causes them to have no interest in hearing what your competitors have to say. The definition of Customer Service is simple:

Meet unmet needs all the time, every day in every way.

THE POINT

You can only grow as a seller if you don't lose the business you have already fought to gain.

Way back in Tool #1 in which we covered determining customer needs, I wrote of my failure to renew existing business as well as I should have when I was a rookie sales person at Josten's/American Yearbook Company. Any salesperson who fails to maintain current accounts cannot ultimately succeed.

The best way to maintain your current book of business is to care for it. STUN continues to make the difference but only if the seller recognizes that "old" unmet needs mutate and "new" unmet needs arise.

Customer satisfaction is formulaic: Satisfaction is the intersection of expectations and reality.

Customers have a certain set of expectations. Vendors, like us, deliver products or services. When the products or services delivered are below the set expectations, then the customer is unhappy. What is delivered must match customer expectations exactly. That makes customers happy.

Often I hear corporations talk about "Exceeding Customer Expectations." That's a dangerous path. Why? Because when the products or services we deliver exceed the expectations of the customer and they, as a result, say, "Wow!" they simultaneously raise their expectations for the future.

I am a lifetime Platinum Member of the Marriott Rewards Honored Guest Program. To earn that distinction, I had to stay at a Marriott corporate flagged property 75 nights in a year for several — I actually don't know how many — years. As a Platinum Guest, I receive a bounty of benefits.

[231]

1. The first is a special telephone number to call for reservations. From my experience, it is always answered promptly — more promptly than the regular Marriott telephone reservation line. I expect that to happen and when it does happen I am satisfied.

2. The second benefit is the "Ultimate Reservation Guarantee." If they fail to honor my reservation, they will pay for my accommodations that night at a nearby hotel and compensate me for my inconvenience. This is an interesting standard to offer. It says, "We know that sometime we are going to fail. We won't have the room we promised you because someone else is in it. We're going to find you a room and give you some money when that happens." I don't know whether or not they will get a "Wow!" from me on this one because the idea that a reserved room won't be available is a major service failure — a failure to meet my expectations. It is difficult to recover from such a thing and even finding me a room someplace else and giving me some money is probably not going to make me happy.

3. The third benefit — and the one I value most — is the "48-Hour Guaranteed Availability" promise. They guarantee that if I call to make a reservation at least 48 hours before my arrival at any of their "participating" hotels, they guarantee me a room even if the hotel is "sold out." I take that to mean they will bump someone else if I use this benefit. That meets my expectations, but assures the fact that someone else's expectations will not be met. One customer is satisfied and one is certainly not satisfied. Why do that? I assume they will try to bump an occasional traveler and accommodate me, the frequent traveler, because I have a greater lifetime customer value for them. The problem with this guarantee is in the details. First, it only applies to "participating" properties and second, if "may not be available during certain limited dates or special events." When I have called and told my 48-Hour Guarantee Availability is not available, I am highly dissatisfied because I had come to count on it. It was what I expected. Delivering me my guaranteed room satisfies me, denying me my reservation 48 hours in advance dissatisfies me. Moments like that encourage me — in fact, they force me — to take my business to a competitor. Marriott hopes the competitor disappoints me so that I will come back.

The reason I offered you that lengthy explanation of what Marriott does is this: They have raised my expectations. That means they must do better just to satisfy me. I am not going to say "Wow!" for something I expect; only something beyond what I expect. So, while I love that they offer me extra benefits, woe be it to them should they fail to deliver. My disappointment will be of their own making because they voluntarily took the risk to raise my expectations.

My friends at Anheuser-Busch always boasted about their higher levels of customer service — levels better than retailers would expect from Miller or Coors. They generally were correct about this in that retailers expected more from the "Bud Man." The problem with that was that when Miller or Coors delivered service below what Anheuser-Busch delivered,

retailers tended to forgive it because they didn't expect as much from Miller or Coors. In effect, A-B was penalized for being better because the competition got away with failings that A-B could not get away with.

I saw it so much. The A-B salesperson would be pitching several new SKUs of one of their brands resulting from a packaging innovation. Maybe it would be eight-packs of 16 ounce cans that were introduced as a new package to supplement the existing six-packs and twelve-packs of 16 ounce cans the retailer was already carrying. The retailer saw the benefit of the new package because it hit a desirable price point that the twelve-packs could not achieve and offered the benefit of an incremental sale that might otherwise be lost. The Bud Man had only to find a place to put this new package in a beer section that had no empty space. The Bud Man, therefore, had to displace a competitor's package. Maybe he would say, "Well, let's take out that twelve-pack of Miller High Life. It doesn't sell very well."

The retailer would say something like, "Yeah but I hate to take space away from the Miller guy; he doesn't have much space to begin with."

The Bud Man would say, "True but that's because his beer doesn't sell very quickly. Plus, he doesn't service the space he has as well as he should." The implication of these two facts — and they were true in the situation I now recount — was that Miller was failing to live up to the expectation that the retailer ought to have and would have if those facings were assigned to A-B.

"Yeah, but they're smaller. I don't expect as much from them as I expect from you," the retailer would say. Ouch. A-B was being penalized because they were better at servicing this retailer's store and better at brewing and advertising a beer that the consumer wanted than was Miller. But, Miller was actually being rewarded for being "less good" because the retailer was expecting less from Miller to begin with. To satisfy a customer, all you have to do is meet their expectations and their expectations are largely set by you.

In the retail business, I have learned to expect more from Nordstrom or Neiman Marcus than I expect from Macy's or JCPenney. Even when each of these offers me the identical product — say Ralph Lauren dresses — at the same or similar prices, I expect more from those who have taught me that they pride themselves on delivering more. Given the choice, when the price is the same or nearly so, I will buy the item from Nordstrom or Neiman's because I feel as though it is somehow better to do so.

However, when Macy's offers me the same goods at a lower price, my loyalty wanes and I opt to save the money.

Therefore, the problem for Nordstrom or Neiman's occurs when Macy's or JCPenney offers the same goods at a lower price. Nordstrom or Neiman's must convince me they are offering better service — or better something — or I will not pay them a premium.

Now consider this situation in the online world. Countless bricks and mortar retailers have gone under as their online competitors have grown. These older entities served as showrooms for shoppers where they could kick the tires, touch and feel the product only to return home to buy online at a lower price. As UPS and FedEx have improved their home delivery speed and efficiency, this has become more and more true.

Bottom line, as consumers, we must perceive that our unmet need is being better or more completely met if we are to pay more for "the same thing."

The only way traditional bricks and mortar retailers will win against internet-based competitors is if they create higher expectations and then meet them. Their challenge — and it is a big one — is to figure out how to do that. And, if they ever fail to measure up to the new expectation, they will lose the customer not once but forever. Therein lies the risk in setting unrealistic expectations that cannot be consistently met.

Many traditional enterprises have determined that competing against the internet upstarts is not, over the long term, feasible. Rather than decline and expire, they have decided to launch online offerings of their own. Surely, this is critical for their survival as technology redefines what we sellers offer to satisfy the unmet needs of customers and markets.

In the airline business, Southwest pioneered the idea of reducing customer expectations and then delivering exactly at that reduced level. For example, Southwest doesn't assign seats. If you expect assigned seats you are going to be disappointed by Southwest's service. But they tell you not to expect that so, you don't. Southwest, even back when airlines routinely served food, served nothing more than a tiny bag of peanuts. If you expected lunch, you were going to be disappointed by Southwest's service. But, they told you in advance to not expect that so, you didn't.

[235

Southwest satisfied their customers by doing less for them. It worked because their customers expected less from them. How did that come to pass? Southwest promised one other thing: Lower fares. Customers of Southwest tolerated one service "failure" because they valued a different promise more: Lower ticket prices. Southwest set the expectation and delivered on it precisely. They grew and grew and grew and satisfied millions of passengers because they did that and more.

Southwest actually over delivered on the in-flight experience. One way they did it was to, for the most part, deliver a fun flight through the efforts on extroverted and highly-satisfied flight attendants. Other airlines might populate their flight attendant ranks with grouchy people, but not Southwest. As a frequent flyer, I expected many things and among them was a "nice" flight attendant. From time to time every airline failed me on that expectation, but Southwest failed infrequently while the other "majors" failed more frequently. I flew Southwest a lot because of that. They met my expectations and satisfied me more often than their competition did.

Southwest flight attendants communicate their approach to customer service through their friendly attitudes. This whole notion of communication raises another important point about customer service. On assignment for Anheuser-Busch in the early 1990s, I was sent to Memphis, TN, to attend a Federal Express Quality "School."

The Company won the Malcom Baldridge Quality Award and did some amazing things with Quality of Service Indicators and more. Anyway, while there, I became a fan of the founder of the company, Fred Smith. I will quote Fred Smith on one point regarding customer service here. He said, "The sun will never set on a customer inquiry." He meant that if a customer called with a question, that customer would get an answer by the end of that day. The answer might be, "We don't have an answer yet," but it would be an answer.

236]

That simple pledge has stuck with me. Customer service in this instance is about communication. If you receive an email or a call or a text from a customer, you must acknowledge receipt of that communication... even if your acknowledgement is that you don't yet have an answer or a solution but that you are working on it.

In this day of email and text strings, this point is more important than it ever was because the dialog between customer and supplier is archived for all to later see.

If your customer calls, emails, texts, faxes or smoke-signals with a question or concern, reply saying that you have received that question or concern and that you are working on it. Do not, under any circumstance, skip this step and go to work solving the problem. Your customer won't know that you are doing that and will wonder what is happening. Communication is a key component to customer retention and acknowledgement that there is an issue on the table is critical.

Another key communication point is all about style. A CEO friend of mine enlisted the services of a real estate agent for the purpose of selling a house. That agent made a stellar listing presentation — I was there to witness it.

Later, when the CEO client had questions or concerns, the agent would reply — usually promptly — but with a minimum of information. This particular CEO was a High D type (many CEOs are) and began to sour on the agent, primarily because of the way he communicated.

He would answer the question posed but fail to add context, a recommendation of additional details that would have helped the CEO to understand better what was happening with the sale of that home.

One of my favorite quotes is, "Don't bring me problems; bring me solutions." If you do research on this philosophy you will find endorsements and condemnations about its advisability. In this situation, the quote is correct. The real estate agent is the expert on the issue of selling a home and the CEO is not. The real estate agent should, whenever pointing out an issue to this person, accompany that issue with a recommendation for action.

[237]

"You are not getting any showings," should be accompanied by the supposed reason why: "because the listing price is too high." Then, that statement should be followed by a recommendation: "To get more showings, we should reduce the selling price by five percent. I believe that, by doing so, we will place your home inside the constraints of more buyers and will draw them to see and consider buying your property."

The problem of "no showings" is in that way put in context "price too high" and a recommendation is attached "reduce the price" which is supported by an expert opinion about an outcome "more showings" leading to the desired outcome "sell the house."

Out of context and without the additional communication, the CEO quickly lost respect for the agent and when a High D loses respect for someone, the relationship is often irrevocably broken. Had he studied the CEO's personality a bit and taken just two minutes more when writing emails, he would have maintained that critical respect and would have been given more time to market the home. When it did not sell quickly, instead of blaming him, the CEO would have blamed the market, the price, or some other thing rather than blaming him, a person.

If you want your customer relationship to thrive, "don't bring your customer problems without putting the problem into context and accompanying it with a recommended course of action supported by an anticipated result."

And, never assume that a one sentence text or email will be well received. Without voice tone and body language, that communication is certainly going to be misinterpreted. Take this sample sentence, "said" in nine different tones:

- "I didn't say the price was too high."
  That's a simple sentence with a clear meaning. Or, is it?

- "I didn't say the price was too high,"
  with the emphasis on the word I means that
  I didn't say it; perhaps someone else did.

- "I DIDN'T say the price was too high,"
  is simply a denial of having said it.

- "I didn't SAY the price was too high,"
  means that while I did not utter the words
  I certainly may have implied it in other ways.

- "I didn't say THE price was too high,"
  means that the price of the house isn't at issue,
  it is more about the history of price decreases
  over time that hurt the chance to sell the home.

- "I didn't say the PRICE was too high," means that I did say something else such as the cabinets needed to be repainted or the step-down from the front door was perceived negatively by potential buyers.

- "I didn't say the price WAS too high," means that it wasn't too high under former market conditions but it certainly is too high now.

- "I didn't say the price was TOO high," means that while the price is a bit high, it is not a lot too high.

- "I didn't say the price was too HIGH," means that the amount of the price is OK but that something else about the price is problematic such as current interest rates making interest costs too high for a particular buyer or some other issue.

If the agent had called the CEO and said the sentence over the phone, with voice tone intact, the meaning would have been clearer. By texting or emailing the sentence without supporting facts, the CEO is left with up to eight ways to misunderstand the meaning of the sentence. That is an unacceptable risk taken by a seller when a relationship and a commission are on the line.

[239

For you to grow as a seller, you must communicate well and meet your customers' expectations day in and day out. If you cannot deliver something that your competitor can deliver then you had best be clear about that from the onset of your relationship. And, you will be forced to come up with a compensating offering which exceeds your competitor's ability to deliver if you want to prosper.

But, don't think that exceeding your customer's expectations is the way to go. Meeting their expectations — meeting their needs — is the way to go. The only benefit you will gain from "going the extra mile" is a fleeting "Wow!" followed by an expectation that the extra mile you went will no longer be thought of as extra in the future. In the future, it will be expected.

I drive a BMW. I love the car. It delivers exactly what I expect from it. It never "Wows" me because I expect it to do what it does. It can't do more. The dealership where I have it serviced delivers good service and I expect that because they promise me that they will do that.

However, each time I complete a service experience with my BMW, I get a satisfaction survey. I am told by the dealership people that if I don't feel that they delivered a "10" on every survey item then they consider themselves (and BMW corporate considers them) as failing. My problem is that the definition of "10" is "Exceeds Expectations." That is wrong on so many levels that it makes me angry every time I get a survey.

I expect more from BMW. They deliver more. That makes me a satisfied customer. They cannot consistently exceed my already high expectations without ultimately "expecting" themselves right out of business.

Every time I am asked to give them an "Exceeds Expectations" rating it angers me. They are asking me to lie and I don't like it. They shouldn't demand that my expectations be exceeded. They should only demand that their service standards be higher than their competition and that their dealers meet that higher service standard every time. That's a win for them. And, it is something they can sustain. And as for me, I don't have to lie every time to make the dealership somehow look better in the eyes of the BMW Company.

I have read lots of books about Customer Satisfaction. Many of them tell story after story of how an employee wildly exceeded customer expectations and was rewarded for that with money and a plaque and their picture in the employee newsletter. The problem with that is that other hard working employees who weren't put in the same situation couldn't match that behavior.

Here's an example. I read of a Ritz Carlton Hotel customer whose luggage was lost and who needed a suit to wear for a critical meeting the next day. You guessed it: The desk clerk just happened to be the same size and went home and got one of his personal clean suits and brought it to the guest to wear for the meeting. I think that is wonderful and worthy of money and a plaque and a picture in the paper. But, when we use it as an example of what other employees should do, we create a danger. I admire the employee's commitment to going the extra mile for the customer, but I fear the expectation set by this example.

All of those employees who aren't the right size or who don't have a clean suit at home or live too far away or who just don't like to share their clothes with strangers are going to be looked down upon when the next guest shows up without a suit for the next day's meeting.

[241]

Imagine the scenario. My luggage is lost. I check in. The front desk associate is a female. I ask if there is a male associate about my size who could check me in because I need to borrow his suit. Ridiculous? Not as ridiculous as it sounds because I have read the story about the other guy and the other front desk person and I think that's what I have a right to expect at the Ritz Carlton. I would never expect that at the Marriott because they have never touted such a story even if one actually did happen. Raising customer expectations by telling "Wow" stories is dangerous.

"Well, you did it for that other guy; why not me?"

Instead, tell people what you are capable of doing and that you will do exactly that and then do it. Forget about all this hoopla regarding going the extra mile... unless you expect to go that extra mile every time from now on.

One of my favorite phrases is "underpromise and overdeliver." I love that. But, I offer up a bit of caution. With a first time customer, underpromising could cause you to lose a sale that you might have otherwise gotten if you told that customer exactly what you were going to do rather than something less. What if your competition out-promises you and you never get the chance to overdeliver? With a repeat customer to whom you overdelivered last time, you will no longer be allowed to underpromise because they are going to expect that you will deliver at least what they got from you last time.

The key is to understand exactly, precisely and absolutely what their unmet need is and then STUN them. Nothing more.

How do you do that? You follow the psychological Circle of every ethical sale.

They need something. You've got a product or service for which you charge a fair price. You communicate that product or service briefly and then you expand on what that product or service actually does for this customer and how what it does meets their need. You STUN them. The unmet need is now met. There is no reason to exceed that in order to satisfy your customer.

What of those who say you should strive to "delight" your customer by going the extra mile. Fine, I say. Just please know that next time whatever was the "extra mile" this time will not be "extra" next time.

It will be expected and you are the cause for that. You didn't STUN by satisfying the unmet need. You decided to STUN by over-satisfying the unmet need. Next time, they'll expect you to do that again. If it cost you more to over-satisfy, you have now permanently added a cost to doing business with this customer. Be careful here.

As I first mentioned in Tool #6, years ago, I was introduced to Maslow's Hierarchy of Needs. Abraham Maslow, who died in 1970 of a heart attack while jogging at the young age of 62, quoting from Wikipedia now, Maslow was best known "for creating Maslow's hierarchy of needs, a theory of psychological health predicated on fulfilling innate human needs in priority." I saw his theory illustrated in a pyramid and something clicked for me.

STUN is an extension of Maslow's Hierarchy. On his pyramid, the most basic of human needs formed the base and were labeled as basics. Those basics included air, food and water; the basics of life. People needed those most urgently or, said another way, those were the most urgent unmet needs of all human beings. In selling, the base of the pyramid, as expressed by many customers is: The lowest price. For me, the most interesting observations I can make about this is that in today's world most suppliers have worked hard to get their prices down as low as they possibly can. Sure there are exceptions but I'll not discuss that philosophy of value here. So, if you and your competition have shaved your price with the sharpest of razors, I will maintain that need to be met.

Maslow said that when a need was met, more of what met it was no longer valued. For humans, if you have air to breathe, someone who offers you more air doesn't really do much to benefit you. That need, once met, is no longer a motivator. In sales, low prices are like air. Once delivered at the highest level, even lower prices deliver an unsustainable feature and, in fact, bring about suspicion regarding quality. "You get what you pay for," is a slogan known to virtually all of us.

In the Kansas City area, I graduated from Ruskin High School. I asked my English teacher why the school was named Ruskin and she used my question as an excuse to get me to write an essay: Who Was Ruskin.

It turns out that my school was named for John Ruskin, an English art critic and social thinker who died in 1900. I thought that most obscure and got interested in why this guy warranted a high school named for him. I started reading some of his writing. Among his quotes (some sources question that is was really his) was one that stuck in my mind as a consumer.

He allegedly said, "It's unwise to pay too much, but it's worse to pay too little. When you pay too much, you lose a little money - that's all. When you pay too little, you sometimes lose everything, because the thing you bought was incapable of doing the thing it was bought to do. The common law of business balance prohibits paying a little and getting a lot - it can't be done. If you deal with the lowest bidder, it is well to add something for the risk you run, and if you do that you will have enough to pay for something better."

Bless you, Ruskin. Once I adjusted my thinking from high school consumer to adult sales person, I quoted him countless times when customers gave me the price objection. Paul Wineman — my inspiration for the earlier discussed concept of "No, But, If" taught me, "Always defend your price." I used Ruskin to do that and he served me very well time and time again. What his philosophy did was help me get my customers to realize that their pyramid base need of "lower prices" was already met and it was time to move up to the next level where the next most urgent unmet need awaited us.

For Maslow, after basics, the next most human need was security.

For me, on the sales hierarchy, is service. We need to meet their service expectations. Once we've met those requirements, their unmet need is now met and no longer motivates. From my experience, a lot of buyers think the business part of buying is now finished and they ill-advisedly, rise to the next pyramid level to the need for "stuff." In the grocery channel, it used to be that store managers were looking for tickets to the ballgame and bar owners wanted another beer neon sign that often times went into their recreation room at home. This is a sad commentary that sellers could not really address but buyers' bosses could. I am reminded of strict rules that were created at the highest level of management of many organizations that banned goodies such as this. Thanks, home office. Good move.

After "stuff" on the selling pyramid, then what?

I think it is "ideas." Call me naïve but I think I am right. Buyers begin to trust us once they know our price is fair and our service always

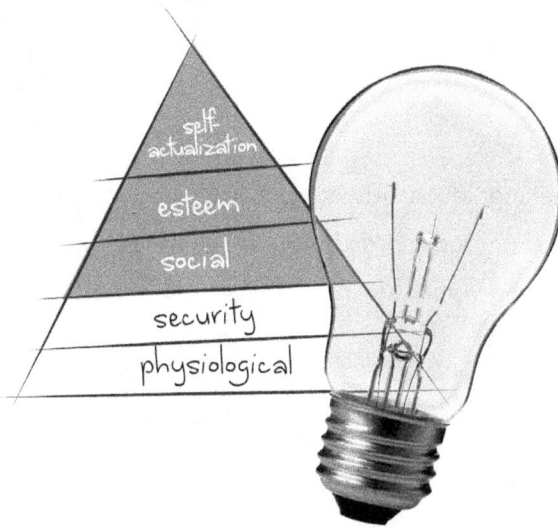

meets their needs. With a bit of prodding from us, we can get them to think about using our brains as well as our backs. They can pick our brains for ideas. We talk to lots of people who use our products and services and maybe, just maybe, we've gained some insight from those folks which could benefit this buyer. When you, as a seller, begin to STUN them with ideas, you have vaulted yourself into a brand new level of prestige. In the Anheuser-Busch business I clearly remember when we stopped selling beer and started selling how on-premise retailers could use beer to grow average transaction sizes. It was a revelation. I preached it and preached it and, with a lot of input from many others, the Bud Men got to be very good at it. Since their competition was still stuck on service or "stuff," many Bud Men were clearly different and this difference helped them to become the preferred vendor.

I ended up using this same philosophy with Pepsi, Dr Pepper Snapple, Dolly Madison, Sara Lee and many others. Institutionally altering the way they were viewed by customers with whom they adopted this philosophy. It was very rewarding for me. But it also made sense for my clients. Each of these companies had a quality product offered at a fair price and delivered with great attention to their customers' requirements. It was time for each of them to move up and nobody wanted to just spend a ton of money on box seats. Ideas took over. Selling became less product-based and more business consultative. So cool; I absolutely love this approach.

And, selling ideas has a very low product cost, no inventory expense, no cost of credit, precious extra labor cost. Ideas are, in many cases, free. But, the value they add is worth "a ton of money."

Careful and precise execution of STUN at the idea level vaults you, ultimately, to the top of my sales pyramid: Partnership. You are no longer thought of as a mere vendor. You are a partner in profitability for them.

I love STUN when, over time, the unmet need becomes more sophisticated. And, thinking about it in parallel to Maslow got me there. It can get you there too. But, be cautious. You cannot remain balanced at the top of a pyramid if the base crumbles. You've got to continue with the fair price for the required quality of product and the service level that matches what your customer needs. Become the expert. It's fun.

How do you stay current? Survey your customers. When, in the past, we have done those surveys, we find that customers want, first and foremost, to be called upon by intelligent and thoughtful sellers. Next, they want a competitive price followed by reliable delivery, followed by accurate stocking, accurate invoicing, good merchandising, things that help them sell the product they sell to the people they ultimately call their customers.

So, how smart are you. If you've made it this far in STUN, you're smarter than you were before you started. At least, I hope so. Of course, there's more. Think about what your customer does to be profitable. What can you do to help them on the revenue side of their business? Once you have finished helping them minimize expenses—which is what your competition matches you on day in and day out — it is unwise to just stop and continue doing what you have always done. Remember Einstein. You can't grow if you keep doing what you have always done.

Do the thing that moves up the selling pyramid. Become not only a supplier of things; become a supplier of ideas. Your point of difference is that you are the smart one, the creative one.

[247

Understand customer needs, speak customer, use the philosophical Circle (you need this, I've got this and it does this which is what you need) and maintain that. Solve problems. Empathize, apologize and fix things that go awry. Then, deliver ideas.

WHAT I WOULD HAVE DONE DIFFERENTLY
IF I KNEW THEN WHAT I KNOW NOW

My territory management system would have been much more disciplined in that I would have set up a much higher call frequency for existing accounts. My goals for those accounts would have been to refresh my understanding of the unmet needs of each account so that I could better practice STUN with each of them. As I planned my sales volume and income goals, I would have been much more cognizant of the contributions made by those who I may have taken for granted.

WHAT YOU SHOULD DO RIGHT NOW

Get out your calendar. Decide how you are going to budget your time. Weigh "maintain" vs. "gain" to determine how you need to allocate time to existing customers.

Perfect your process for not simply uncovering your customers' unmet needs but for validating and updating them. Never, ever take any account for granted. Know where your competition is and upon whom they are calling. Understand the true negative objections that may exist in your accounts. Perfect the process of weighing the positives you offer against the positives your competition will aim at your negatives.

Assume nothing when it comes to re-signing your existing business. You assume at your own growth peril.

For more on this topic, review "Customer Service Later" in the ej4 video, "Customer Service Basics" at STUNselling.com/customer_service.

[249

SECTION THREE

When **STUN** Fails

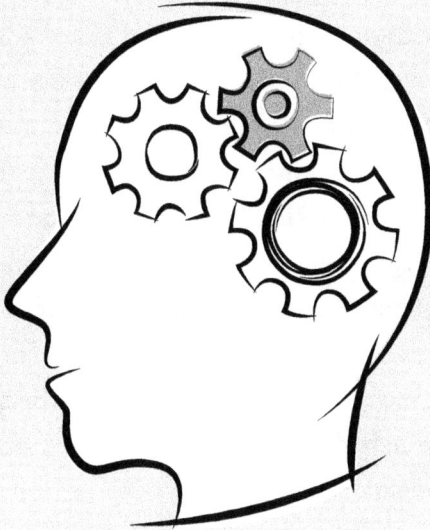

Here's What You're Going to Learn

STUN is the greatest sales "system" I've ever tried.
I believe in it with all my heart.
It has delivered me success after success after success.
Yet, it is doomed to fail under certain circumstances.

THE POINT

Nothing is perfect. If STUN doesn't work, you may be able to diagnose why not... and, of course, if STUN doesn't work, please try something else! Whatever you do, don't give up on the opportunity.

There are some situations where you need to try something else, try something new or even walk away. But, and I learned this one from Helzberg Diamond Stores, it could be that it isn't working because of you. Re-read the discussion in Tool 9, Handing Tough Customers. Maybe your approach or your personality is doomed to fail with this customer. At Helzberg, when their sales team feels this, they "T.O." the customer, meaning they "Turn Over" the customer to a different sales team member. I had never heard of this until I met Helzberg CEO, Beryl Raff. She set me straight. For them, T.O. works like a charm. If you want to see it in action, go buy a diamond, but behave indifferently toward the first associate. See what happens next. It's fascinating and effective and innovative to see. And, chances are, you'll end up with a beautiful pair of diamond studs in the process!

STUN will fail if your prospect will absolutely, under no circumstance, allow you to understand what his unmet need is. You can't STUN if you don't know UN. Why would a prospect be that closed? They don't trust you, they think their unmet need is none of your business or they don't want you to win — they want you to fail and they are going to do everything in their power to foil you. Go back and re-review Tool #1. If that doesn't help, T.O. If that's not possible, move on. There is money to be made down the street.

STUN will fail if you insist on wowing your customer with your own jargon. Take another look at Tool #2.

STUN will fail if you don't pick up the pace. Refresh your knowledge of Tool #3.

STUN will fail if you dwell on features and skim over benefits. Remember, they aren't buying what you're selling. They're buying what you're selling will do for them. Cut back on features if you must but never cut back on benefits. Address this with Tool #4.

[253

STUN will fail if you expect your prospect to adapt to your personality. They won't. Since they won't, you must. Adopt the High D tactics when selling to a High D but don't use those tactics when you are selling to a High I, High S or High C. Understand customer personalities by re-reading Tool #5.

STUN will fail if you sell to a user with economic features and benefits. And, it will fail if you sell to a specifications oriented technical buyer with user benefits. Brush up on Tool #6.

STUN will fail if you don't close. Reread, reread and reread Tool #7.

STUN will fail if you let objections get you down. Objections are your best friend if you know how to classify and then deal with them. They get you to another close more quickly. We address objections with Tool #8.

STUN will fail if you allow yourself to be intimidated, and ultimately defeated, by tough customers. Look at Tool #9.

STUN will fail if you walk away when stalled. Reread, reread and reread Tool #10.

STUN won't fail, but you or your employer won't make any money if you allow your customer to nibble you to death. Reread Tool #11.

STUN will fail if you talk when you should be listening. Shut up and reread Tool #12.

STUN will fail if you fail to take into account the perils of rolling out a new product. Look again at Tool #13.

STUN will fail if you cannot bond with your prospect, if they don't like you or if they dread your appointment times. Smile and reread Tool #14.

STUN will fail if you sell it and then go away never to be seen again. Yep, you guessed it, reread Tool #15.

STUN will fail if you are dealing with a customer who is not ethical. The customer who demands that you cheat, steal, collude, price-fix, betray trade secrets or any other unethical behavior is not a person to be STUNned. They should be SHUNned instead.

STUN will fail if, when you fail to deliver on a promise, you subsequently fail to promptly admit it and fix it. We all suffer service or product failures from time to time. This is a truth of the human condition which introduces fallibility into reality. When you fail to deliver, admit it and fix it. Don't fix blame; fix the problem. You may find that STUN works better after a failure than it ever did before the failure occurred if you meet the new unmet need created by the failure to meet the former unmet need. I am amazed by how much more loyal customers are when, after they have been disappointed, the seller accepted blame and culpability and then fixed their problem to their satisfaction — a situation that could not have occurred without the failure that prompted it.

STUN will fail if you are dealing with a customer who will only settle for a win/lose relationship. If you're in a "one and done" business, that may be OK. By one and done I mean this is a customer to whom you are going to sell one time only and never see again. In those situations, customers are likely to try to rip you off and, maybe, you're going to try to do the same thing in return. I have no experience in these businesses and I don't care to. I love finding a customer and then selling to them again and again and again. I built a great life with Pepsi and Anheuser-Busch and MasterCard and UBS and a few others who I trusted and who trusted me in return. There was always value added for price paid. STUN is perfect for that as STUN requires a win/win outcome. I sleep better every night leaving greed in my dust and making sure that my partnership with others makes them want to deal with me again.

[255

At ej4, we had to fire a customer once. It was the best thing we ever did. We lost some money but we gained happiness. I'm just sayin'...

Finally, STUN will fail if you forget this slogan:
"Without a Need, Don't Proceed."

WHAT I WOULD HAVE DONE DIFFERENTLY
IF I KNEW THEN WHAT I KNOW NOW

I would have sought out compatible customers and STUNned them fiercely. I would have sold hard to incompatible customers but, when it was time to leave, I would have left and spent my time and energy and emotion where it would bring me and my employer better end results.

WHAT YOU SHOULD DO RIGHT NOW

Prioritize your time and sell to customers who will maximize what they receive from you and you from them. Only when you have time on your hands should you spend it with win/lose prospects. Life is short and it is best and most profitably spent with people who are ethical, who believe in give and take, compromise for mutual best interest, fairness, ethics and, well, peace on earth.

[257

    Live long and prosper.

STUN Tool Summary

STUN!

People are motivated
by things that Satisfy Their Unmet Needs.

Therefore it stands to reason that they will be motivated to buy when you STUN™ them. That is, Satisfy Their Unmet Need. When you adopt this as your sales process, you'll learn how to turn tough customers into easier customers, how to close faster, how to stop customer nibbling, how to overcome the price objection and much more. You'll be STUNned.

Keep in mind: The only thing your customers really care about is profitability (revenues minus expenses). If you can help them achieve that goal, you are one step closer to closing the sale.

TOOL #1 Determining Customer Needs

"Without a Need, Don't Proceed." If your customer doesn't need what you're selling, you're out of luck; you won't sell anything. If your customer needs what you're selling, you're going to win... and so is your customer. But, you have to do everything right. Therefore, talk less about what you're selling. Talk more about how your customer needs what you're selling and how what you're selling meets or satisfies his need. Remember: Your customer will only buy the solution you are selling because he receives a benefit... and, that only works if the benefit satisfies his unmet need!

TOOL #2 Speaking "Customer"

People are more receptive to sellers who "speak their language" by referring to terms and conditions of the sale using vocabulary familiar and customary to them. Don't talk your talk; talk their talk. Customers appreciate sellers who speak their language. These customers will tell sellers about their problems, what they need, what makes them happy and what is really important to them. They get snippy with salespeople who don't speak their language — in fact, these customers turn up their noses at ignorant sellers, often steering them wrong and treating them as if they are not worthy of the customer's time.

TOOL #3 The QuickSell®

Sales don't have to take a long time. Using the QuickSell methodology, you can close a sale in as few as five seconds.

To Get:	Your customers to buy more quickly
You Should:	Employ the QuickSell Process
Which Would:	Get you to "Yes" or an objection right away
I Could:	Show you how it works

TOOL #4 Turning Features Into Benefits

Translating features into benefits is the first skill that a successful seller must master. However, most training at many companies is actually product-focused (i.e. feature-focused) training, rather than benefit-focused training. Features are boring. Benefits are enticing, motivational and the reason people buy. Talking on and on about product or service features will kill a sale. Talking succinctly about benefits — if they satisfy an unmet need — leads to a faster and better sale.

[261]

TOOL #5 Selling to Different Personality Types

There are four basic personality types that you must sell to: Dominant, Influencer, Steady and Compliant. Your best chance of closing a sale is to recognize the personality type of your buyer and sell to him/her based on the way in which he/she prefers to interact with others. And, when it comes to closing the sale, your personality type as a seller is irrelevant. Instead, focus on your customer — identify his/her primary personality type and sell to that style. You will achieve startlingly superior results.

TOOL #6 Selling to Different Customer Roles

In a complex sale or among the cast members of sale to a committee, different people represent different outlooks on your product or service. One person may be the person who actually uses your product. Another may be the person who determines how your product interacts with other products that the buyer's company already uses. Another may be simply the money person deciding if the price is competitive. Another may have a close relationship with your company while still another may have a close relationship with your competition. These people all look at what you are selling from a different perspective. Most importantly, they each have a different unmet need. You must address all roles and approach each one in a different manner if you hope to close the sale. Don't forget: One set of features and benefits doesn't fit all different buyers inside a single prospect company because they each have different unmet needs. You need to customize your selling story for each person's needs. For each one, without a need, don't proceed.

262]

TOOL #7 Closing the Sale

It's not a sale until it's closed. And, while it is true that there are many, many different ways to close a sale, it is the "set up" for the close that truly makes the difference. To increase your success rate, first set it up, then close. Nod momentum is the key since, if their head is bobbing up and down, it will be difficult for your customer to say "No," and very natural for them to say, "Yes!"

TOOL #8 Overcoming Objections

There are four types of objections you will encounter in sales: Misunderstanding, Doubt, Indifference and True Negative. Each type of objection must be resolved with a different approach in order to close the sale. For each type of objection, there is a unique way to address the customer's concern and turn his/her "No" into a "Yes" so you can close the sale.

TOOL #9 Handling Tough Customers

Tough customers can be sold. In fact, they are the most fun to sell to once you figure out how to do it. What you do is simple really. You pound on their unmet need until they cede the point. Then, you move forward, cautiously, with features and benefits that relate to the unmet need they are willing to acknowledge.

TOOL #10 Defeating Stalls

Most sales professionals are all too familiar with buyers who, rather than making a yes/no decision, simply stall. A stall is neither a "Yes" nor a "No." The problem is that when a stall is accepted, it seldom becomes a "Yes" and often dissolves into a "No." There are two different types of stalls: 1) "Let me think about it" and 2) "I'll have to talk to someone else before I can give you an answer" (typically referred to as the "Committee Stall"). Both can be defeated but may require some pre-planning.

TOOL #11 No, But, If™

Once a prospect accepts that he might actually buy what you are selling, if he is good, he will begin to nibble away at you. He will ask for a concession in terms such as a better price or a quicker delivery or a slower payment date. If you allow him to take that first bite, he will nibble again and again until you stop him. Why wouldn't he? It's working. To stop the nibbling, you must nibble back. You do that by never saying "Yes" to a nibble. Instead, even if the nibble is one you are willing to concede, you must say "No. I can't do that. But, I can do this IF you will do that." No, But, If works wonders.

TOOL #12 When to Shut Up

Selling is not about talking. Selling is not presenting. Selling is about engaging in a conversation. It's a dialog rather than a monologue. Talking and presenting can only stop when you are willing to engage in silence. Customers are not engaged unless they are talking. For them to talk, you have to shut up. But, how do you know when to shut up? You shut up on buying signs.

TOOL #13 Selling in New Products

It might seem as though it would be easier to sell in a new product to an existing customer, but reality is often just the opposite. Be prepared! Sure, you already have a relationship with a customer, but when the marketing people suddenly announce there is a new product for you to sell, it may be more difficult than you anticipate. The way you get that second or twenty-second product or service into the customer's inventory isn't the same as how you sold in the first one.

TOOL # **14** Smile

People like to buy from people they like. People like people who smile. Regardless of your personality, you need to smile at people even if it hurts. Please, note, however that the size of your smile depends not on your mood but upon the personality of whoever is viewing it.

TOOL # **15** Customer Service Later

To grow, you cannot rely solely on new business. You can only grow as a seller if you don't lose the business you have already fought to gain. You must maintain what you have in order to gain overall. The way you maintain your current customers is to service their unmet needs with a vigor that causes them to have no interest in hearing what your competitors have to say. The definition of Customer Service is simple: Meet unmet needs all the time, every day in every way.

[265

You can
STUN!

ABOUT THE AUTHOR

Paul Russell is founder and owner of ej4, a professional development organization that is much more than an eLearning company – it offers the tools that allow companies to train, track, share and communicate better. Coupling broadcast television experience with leader-led training as principal at Russell Training Group, Inc., he re-engineered multi-day seminar learning into low-cost, on-line, curriculum-based, short-form, green-screen video learning.

In his spare time, Paul travels the globe and has visited well over 100 countries. Go ahead, ask him his favorite place.

www.ingramcontent.com/pod-product-compliance
Lightning Source LLC
Chambersburg PA
CBHW060336200326
41519CB00011BA/1951